The Economist Intelligence Unit Global Manager

Also Published by McGraw-Hill

Noël Clarke
THE ECONOMIST INTELLIGENCE UNIT GUIDE TO EUROBONDS

Andrea Mackiewicz
THE ECONOMIST INTELLIGENCE UNIT GUIDE TO BUILDING A GLOBAL IMAGE

Shirley B. Dreifus, Editor
BUSINESS INTERNATIONAL'S GLOBAL MANAGEMENT DESK REFERENCE

Thomas J. Ehrbar, Editor
BUSINESS INTERNATIONAL'S GUIDE TO INTERNATIONAL LICENSING

Gray Newman and Anna Szterenfeld
BUSINESS INTERNATIONAL'S GUIDE TO DOING BUSINESS IN MEXICO

The Economist Intelligence Unit Global Manager

Recruiting, Developing, and Keeping World Class Executives

Michael Moynihan

McGraw-Hill, Inc.

New York   San Francisco   Washington, D.C.   Auckland   Bogotá
Caracas   Lisbon   London   Madrid   Mexico City   Milan
Montreal   New Delhi   San Juan   Singapore
Sydney   Tokyo   Toronto

Library of Congress Cataloging-in-Publication Data

Moynihan, Michael, date.
    The Economist Intelligence Unit global manager / Michael Moynihan.
        p.   cm.
    Includes index.
    ISBN 0-07-009351-2 :
    1. Executive ability. 2. Executive—Recruiting. 3. Executives—
Training of. 4. Cross-cultural orientation. 5. International
education. 6. Management—Social aspects. I. Global Intelligence
Unit (New York, N.Y.) II. Title. III. Title: Global manager.
    HD38.2.M69   1993
    658.4'07—dc20   93-1942
                                              CIP

HD38
.2
.M69
1993

1 2 3 4 5 6 7 8 9 0   DOC/DOC   9 9 8 7 6 5 4 3

ISBN 0-07-009351-2

*The sponsoring editor for this book was David Conti, the editing supervisor
was Kimberly A. Goff, and the production supervisor was Pamela A. Pelton.
This book was set in Palatino. It was composed by McGraw-Hill's Professional
Book Group composition unit.*

Printed and bound by R. R. Donnelley & Sons Company.

This book is printed on recycled, acid-free paper containing a
minimum of 50% recycled de-inked fiber.

This publication is designed to provide accurate and authoritative information in regard to the subject matter covered. It is sold with the understanding that the publisher is not engaged in rendering legal, accounting,
or other professional service. If legal advice or other expert assistance is
required, the services of a competent professional person should be
sought.
—From the declaration of principles jointly adopted by a committee of the
American Bar Association and a committee of publishers

Contents

Preface

Corporate executives who can operate effectively across cultures and borders are emerging as key factors in the battle for global corporate success. As the world grows ever smaller, improved cross-cultural skills and an international perspective are critical executive qualities. In the industrialized countries, a tightening labor market resulting from the steady aging of the work force will create a shortage of qualified executives in the coming decade. Thus, as more and more companies expand abroad, competition for top talent to run new international operations will steadily intensify. To meet these challenges, companies must develop new ways to cultivate international executive talent and to hold on to that talent, once they have invested in it. Companies must design training programs for both local nationals and expatriates to give new managers the skills to compete on a new international playing field.

The Economist Intelligence Unit Global Manager shows how international companies train their international executives. Addressed primarily to executives responsible for managing the quality and productivity of the international work force, this study is designed to help firms attract, train and retain highly qualified and motivated employees. The report examines techniques used by leading firms to enable their executives to operate effectively throughout the world. In addition, the study describes recruitment and screening practices and identifies which career-path strategies work best to heighten employee commitment to the international side of business.

Research Methodology

The Economist Intelligence Unit Global Manager is the result of extensive original research into the management-development practices of major companies in North America, Europe and Asia. The firms selected span various industries, including computers, consumer electronics, chemicals, automobiles, beverages, industrial components, medical equipment and packaging. In preparing this book, the Economist Intelligence Unit interviewed over 30 executives managing international human resources at distinguished multinational companies. Through these interviews, the Economist Intelligence Unit obtained valuable firsthand information about how various strategies have worked, under which conditions and where. In addition to interviewing corporate executives, the Economist Intelligence Unit also spoke with various consultants and educators. Finally, the Economist Intelligence Unit also made use of several studies covering training, management development and repatriation practices around the world.

Acknowledgments

The Economist Intelligence Unit wishes to thank all the corporate executives, consultants, educators and other experts whose generous assistnace and gracious cooperation made this book possible.

The project was undertaken by the Economist Intelligence Unit's Multinational Management unit in New York.

Company Profiles

AT&T. Headquartered in New York City. The company provides products, systems and services in telecommunications and information movement and management worldwide. AT&T employs about 276,000 people and has a direct presence or distributorship in over 200 countries and territories.

Acer Inc. Headquartered in Lungtan, Taiwan. The company is a rapidly growing producer of personal computers. It also markets a range of computer-related services. With over 20 overseas subsidiaries in North America, Western Europe and Asia, Acer employs over 5,600 people worldwide.

Atlas Copco AB. Headquartered in Stockholm. The company is a major manufacturer of specialized industrial machinery in three major product areas—compressor technique, construction and mining technique and industrial technique. Atlas Copco has 20,500 employees worldwide.

Bull SA. Headquartered in Paris. The company is a manufacturer of computers, specializing in integrated systems and networks, with an emphasis on administration, industry, finance and communications equipment. Bull employs about 40,000 people.

The Coca-Cola Co. Headquartered in Atlanta, Georgia. A major global marketer of soft drinks and juice-based beverages. Products include Coca-Cola, Diet Coke, Sprite and Fanta Orange. Juice-based beverages are marketed primarily under the Minute Maid and Hi-C trademarks. The company operates in nearly 170 countries and employs approximately 21,000 people.

Colgate-Palmolive. Headquartered in New York City. The company is a leading global marketer of consumer-based products and services, e.g. Colgate toothpaste, Palmolive soap, Fab detergent, Ajax cleaner and Science Diet pet food. Colgate markets in over 160 countries and employs 24,000 people.

Dow Chemical Co. Headquartered in Midland, Michigan. The company manufactures and supplies more than 2,000 products, including chemicals and performance products, plastics, hydrocarbons and energy and consumer specialties, including agricultural products and pharmaceuticals. Dow employs about 62,000 people.

Fuji Xerox Co Ltd. Headquartered in Tokyo. A 50:50 joint venture between Fuji Photo Film Co Ltd and Rank Xerox Ltd of the UK (Rank Xerox is 51% owned by Xerox Corp of the US), Fuji Xerox produces a wide range of office and office-related equipment, from copiers to workstations and Japanese-language word processors. Fuji Xerox employs 13,765 worldwide.

Fujitsu America Inc. Headquartered in San Jose, California. Established in 1968, Fujitsu American Inc (FAI) is the largest overseas subsidiary of Tokyo-based Fujitsu Ltd, a global leader in computer, telecommunications and semiconductor technologies. FAI's divisions and six domestic subsidiaries develop, design, manufacture, market and support a broad range of computer and telecommunications systems. The company operates over 150 facilities in 33 states and Canada, including four manufacturing plants. FAI has nearly 5,000 employees.

General Electric. Headquartered in Fairfield, Connecticut. GE is a diverse company involved in a wide range of industries, including financial services, plastics, aircraft engines, NBC television, medical systems, lighting, industrial and power systems, appliances, aerospace, communications and services, electrical distribution and control, motors and transportation systems.

General Motors. Headquartered in Detroit. GM is the world's largest industrial company, with automotive operations in 40 countries, which account for nearly 20% of the vehicles sold in the world's competitive markets. In addition to designing, manufacturing and selling cars, trucks and engines, GM competes with the world's automotive parts manufacturers to supply components to the GM vehicle divisions and also to all of the world's car manufacturers and service parts distributors.

IBM Co. Headquartered in Armonk, New York. The company is a major manufacturer of computers and related products for business, government, science, space exploration, defense, education and medicine.

Matsushita Electric Industrial Co Ltd. Headquartered in Osaka, Japan. Matsushita Electric Industrial Co (MEI) is the world's largest electronics manufacturer, with over 120 subsidiaries and affiliates in 38 countries. Products include video equipment, electronic components, home appliances and communication and industrial equipment. Brand names include National, Panasonic, Technics and Quasar. MEI employs 67,700 persons worldwide.

Mitsui & Co. Headquartered in Tokyo. The company is one of Japan's leading (and the oldest) general trading corporations. IT carries out export-import and offshore trade in iron and steel products, nonferrous metals, machinery, chemicals, foods and energy-related products. But the firm is also heavily involved in commercial development, technology transfer and finance and investment. A core member of the Mitsui Group, Mitsui & Co itself has over 200 overseas subsidiaries and over 170 overseas offices. It has nearly 12,000 employees.

NCR Corp. Headquartered in Dayton, Ohio. The company provides a full range of information systems and products worldwide and manufactures computers, other data processing equipment, media products and paper products. NCR operates 20 subsidiaries in over 120 countries and has 55,000 employees.

NEC Corp. Headquartered in Tokyo. Established in 1899, NEC is one of the world's leading providers of computers and industrial electronic systems, home electronics, electron devices and communications equipment. It has a total of 76 consolidated subsidiaries, 58 in Japan and 18 overseas. Besides 62 factories maintained by NEC and its consolidated subsidiaries in Japan, NEC's majority-owned subsidiaries and other affiliates operate 29 manufacturing facilities in 15 countries. It also maintains 26 liaison offices in 24 countries. The group has over 114,600 employees.

NV Philips' Gloeilampenfabrieken Multinational. Headquartered in Eindhoven, The Netherlands, Philips is one of the world's largest manufacturers of electrical and electronic products. The company's output includes lighting equipment, consumer electronics, household appliances, professional products and systems and electronic components. Philips employs 273,000 people worldwide.

Rank Xerox. Headquartered in Marlow, the UK. The company provides a range of copiers and office systems to meet customers' needs in the creation, printing, copying, distribution, filing and publishing of paper and electronic documents. The company—a joint venture between Xerox Corp and The Rank Organization PLC of the UK—has extensive R&D and manufacturing facilities in the European Community, as well as marketing subsidiaries and distributors in over 80 countries in the EC and throughout the world.

Volvo AB.   Headquarters in Gothenburg, Sweden. Volvo's main operations encompass the development, manufacture and marketing of transportation equipment, but the operations also include the food industry, some trading in goods and services and financing activities. The company sells its broad range of products in 130 countries and produces in 30.

The Economist
Intelligence Unit
Global Manager

1
Overview: The Global Manager

Executive Summary

The 1990s will test the capacities of multinational corporations (MNCs) to react rapidly to global changes in human resources as in all other areas of the company. To some degree, technological improvements, such as computerized executive tracking systems, will help companies organize their international human resources efforts. Nevertheless, traditional human resources methods must be refined, expanded and applied to address new challenges that range from a changing work force profile to the impact of corporate restructuring on existing international business relationships.

Already prized at the highest levels of global companies, international experience on the part of executives will become increasingly critical to business success in coming years. At the same time, however, an increasingly tight labor market will put added pressure on companies to properly manage and develop their international work force. Convinced that executives must learn to think globally and act locally, MNCs are directing their most promising executives toward international development assignments designed to foster a corps of seasoned global managers. As international business success has become synonymous with corporate success, international experience on the part of executives has become identified with upward mobility within the company. In turn, cultivation of international executives has emerged as a key strategic concern for companies.

In the uncertain business climate of the 1990s, the ability to develop and retain a skilled and versatile management corps is emerging as a key measure of MNC performance. Increased global competition, instability in the financial markets, a speedup in the introduction of new technologies and soaring marketing and distribution costs are forcing companies to emphasize productivity as a source of revenue growth. The central message of the executives interviewed for this study is that effective management of a firm's human assets is one of the least costly and most predictable sources of productivity gains. The biggest spoils go to those companies that have learned to reach beyond their home bases to exploit a global pool of executive talent.

Although the level of commitment to the development of global management skills varies, fewer and fewer MNCs still nurture executive talent within their "home" countries alone. Most now use local nationals (LNs) and third-country nationals (TCNs) wherever possible abroad and, increasingly, promote the most promising of these individuals to positions at headquarters.

At Philips, one of Europe's best assimilated global corporations, a successful career is hardly possible without international experience "at a high managerial level," says Dr. J. D. de Leeuw, managing director of the corporate staff bureau. This approach appears to have caught on in the US as well: A recent *Fortune* magazine survey of CEOs who represent the *Fortune* 500 found that nearly half had had some international supervisory exposure before assuming the top posts in their firms. Even in Japan, where a preference for cultural homogeneity lingers in the executive suite, an assignment abroad is assuming greater value. Nippon Electric Corp (NEC), for example, now tells its managers that a foreign posting is not a detour and, in fact, can be a shortcut to the top.

What's Behind the Trend

For today's MNC, it is becoming crucial to develop and foster managers with broad-based international experience. The factors that account for the rise in the value of global management skills include the following:

- *Growing international sales exposure.* Falling trade barriers and the consequent rise in new foreign-sourcing opportunities, together with a push in the mature industrialized markets for untapped customers, have steadily increased the percentage of sales revenues derived from foreign markets. For the average Swiss chemical manufacturer, foreign income now accounts for 90% or more of the total.

At present, Japan's automakers, which already derive half their profits from sales to the US, are moving heavily into Europe. Similarly, in a 1989 survey of 99 US firms by the Coalition for the Advancement of Foreign Languages and International Studies (Caflis), 63% of the firms questioned said they believe the international percentage of sales will increase over the coming decade.

Indeed, a weak dollar has pushed US pharmaceutical companies' percentage of foreign sales to an annual average of nearly 40%. Not surprisingly, these internationally minded sectors share a common appreciation for global management skills and are taking the lead in fashioning the training and succession-planning systems needed to keep their companies operating in a competitive environment.

■ *Broader range of relationships with competitors.* The growth of strategic alliances and other new forms of joint-venture and licensing arrangements requires managers who have the skills to weave complex bureaucratic structures into a seamless whole. Not only is there a mix of corporate cultures with which to contend, there are also sensitivities imposed by the clash of nationalities, languages and laws. The ability to adapt to circumstances that may require a new set of "standard operating procedures" is crucial to the success of these nontraditional relationships. Such skills are rarely developed as effectively at headquarters—where autonomous judgment carries greater bureaucratic risks—as in management posts abroad.

■ *Impact of corporate restructuring moves.* In many industries, the response to global competition has encouraged a trend toward consolidation. The number of mergers and acquisitions in the European Community doubled between 1987 and 1989, mimicking the hot US takeover climate earlier in the 1980s. The larger companies that were created by rationalization moves tend to operate across national boundaries, thereby increasing the demand for executives with cross-cultural exposures. The restructurings in Europe, for example, have sparked stiff competition for the services of experienced TCNs, e.g., the Swedes and the Swiss, who are seen as prototypes of a future "Europeanized," regionally oriented executive class.

■ *Erosion of traditional organizational structures.* For many MNCs, the traditional division of functions along domestic and international lines has given way to a global product orientation. One result of the change is the need for training in international management skills on a much wider basis; many individuals who in years past might have spent their entire careers in their home countries are now more likely to spend at least a few years abroad.

Median Age of Population
1980-2025

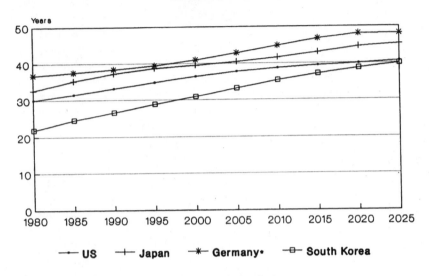

Years

— US   —+— Japan   —*— Germany•   —⊟— South Korea

*data refer to former West Germany

- *Demographic pressures.* Demographic trends show a clear aging of the global work force, particularly in industrialized countries (see graphs pp. 6-7). In Japan, 25% of the population will be over age 65 by 2020, with only slightly lower percentages in the other industrial economies. As more of the postwar "baby boom" generation retire in the early decades of the next century, their ranks will be filled from a far smaller pool of workers, presaging increasingly tight labor markets (see table p. 7).

  Inevitably, companies will be hard pressed to fill many positions, especially if they fail to tap unrecognized talent in distant subsidiaries. Savvy companies already are aware that a global human resources network will be necessary to ensure adequate staffing for future growth.

- *Effect of social change on the workplace.* Companies can no longer depend on a pliant team of experienced—mostly male—managers to fill overseas job vacancies as they arise. "We have to pay more attention to what workers wish to do with their personal life, as well as with their business life," says R. Alicia Whitaker, Colgate-Palmolive's director of management and organization development. "Twenty years ago, the culture of the company was that if you were told to get

Population Aged 60 or More
1980-2025

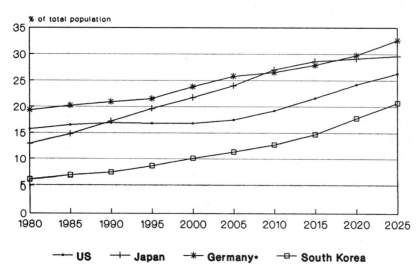

% of total population

—•— US   —+— Japan   —✳— Germany•   —▫— South Korea

•data refer to former West Germany

on a plane and take a foreign assignment, you had to go, but that doesn't work anymore." The rise in dual-career couples has further complicated service abroad. It has limited the pool of available candidates for expatriate transfers, forced companies to look at programs to accommodate or even hire spouses and increased the importance of maintaining the loyalty and skills of LNs.

Age Groups as a % of Total Population 1990–2000

	Aged 20–40		Aged 50+	
	1990	2000	1990	2000
US	33.1	28.6	25.8	28.5
Japan	27.5	27.9	30.1	37.4
EC	30.4	28.8	31.4	34.0
Germany	31.3	27.5	34.0	36.0
France	30.1	27.9	29.7	32.3
Italy	30.2	29.7	32.8	36.0
UK	29.9	28.1	31.3	33.2
Netherlands	32.9	28.9	27.6	32.2

■ *Sensitivities in relations with government.* Although tariffs and other formal trade barriers have declined sharply in recent years, the complexity of doing business abroad has increased markedly. This is the case even in the US, the most open of world markets. Higher taxes and new regulatory strictures in such áreas as the environment and product safety require managers with the ability to be good corporate citizens. This trend has placed new emphasis on the frequently neglected international aspects of corporate staff functions—not only with regard to human resources. Effective international management training today requires that the staff be thoroughly grounded in public relations, legal and other "mediating" skills that can be put to good use abroad.

A Universal Need

Naturally, not all companies are committed to widening their global reach. Does this mean that those firms whose revenue bases remain focused on a single country should not foster a broader international perspective in their management ranks? The answer is a resounding "no," since a strictly domestic perspective ignores the true nature of contemporary competition. Even supposedly secure niches at home have proven vulnerable to foreign inroads. Indeed, the greater a company's dependence on a given niche at home, the greater the threat to overall performance posed by competition from abroad.

This is why an on-site international presence is seen more and more as irrelevant to the need to develop globally minded managers. Competition today *is* global, no matter where it occurs and for virtually any market. Even in a company's backyard, tomorrow's challenge can come from halfway around the world, not just from down the road.

US, European and Japanese MNCs: Different Histories, Different Perspectives

The approaches an MNC takes toward international business, and, specifically, to developing international managers, grow out of its home country's economic and commercial history. For example:

■ *The US.* Despite the perception that US companies are fixated on their enormous domestic market, their reliance on foreign markets is significant—and growing. The book value of US foreign direct investment has risen steadily since the early 1960s, reaching $375 billion in 1989, with almost two thirds in Canada and Western Europe. With this growth in foreign presence, US firms are also becoming aware that they must begin to focus on acquiring managers who can effectively meet the challenges of a globalizing company. For many companies this is requiring a shift in their management styles and perspectives.

From World War II through the end of the 1970s, US management was widely considered the world's best. As a result, rather than adapting to local customs, US MNCs often exerted a strong influence on business practices in the countries where they operated. Impressed with their aura of success, local businessmen sought to emulate US ways of doing business and vied for the chance to cement a relationship with a largely expatriate corps of managers. This gave US MNCs relatively little incentive to learn the ins and outs of the local market.

As their competitive advantage waned, though, US companies found it necessary to pay more attention to the local business culture. Despite significant efforts in this direction, some observers continue to fault US firms for what they see as an excessively domestic orientation. For example, a recent study by the American Society for Training and Development[1] asserts that US executives lack the "careful and complete sensitivity to the diversity of cultures" abroad necessary to compete effectively.

That US managers may find an international assignment daunting is not surprising. Because of the vast size of the domestic market, not only in dollars and people but in miles as well, many US executives may have had little need or chance to interact with people from other countries over the course of their careers. In addition, the high standard of living in the US also made and still makes many assignments abroad less attractive. "We meet a lot of young people who think that going overseas means going to Paris," says Colgate-Palmolive's Whitaker. "In our case, it probably means going to Brazil, the Philippines or maybe Zambia."

The US orientation of both managers and companies is changing and will change even more dramatically over the coming decade as the impact of competition from abroad forces US firms to defend their home markets. In 1989, foreign investments in the US ($400.8 billion) surpassed US holdings abroad. This is driving home the need for a global perspective.

---

[1] Rhinesmith, Stephen H.; Williamson, John H.; Ehlen, David M.; and Maxwell, Denise S., "Developing Leaders for the Global Enterprise," *Training and Development Journal*, April 1989.

Although US firms have reacted slowly, most now realize they must think globally to compete. In its 1989 survey of large US firms, Caflis found that 86% of respondents said they plan to place a "greater emphasis on international competence among management and employees" in the future, both in recruiting and training of existing personnel. Companies cited four primary areas in which increased international competence is particularly important: marketing, foreign personnel recruitment, commercial negotiation with customers and suppliers and strategic planning.

- *Europe.* In contrast to US and Japanese firms, many European companies have an international tradition that dates back to their respective countries' colonial periods. Many European firms currently retain strong ties to markets they first developed decades or even centuries ago. With such deep roots in their overseas markets, these companies have typically accumulated a vast knowledge of local business conditions and practices that newcomers would be hard pressed to duplicate.

    Europe's geographic and cultural diversity implies that the vast majority of European-born executives have at least traveled to other countries, even if they have not worked or lived in them. MNCs based in the smaller European countries, such as the Netherlands' Philips and Switzerland's Nestle, have had to develop international sensitivity and savvy because of their limited domestic markets. With the coming of the European Community's single market in 1992 and the democratization of Eastern Europe, the trend toward truly "European" managers will undoubtedly accelerate. Because of their strong belief in training and their history of working in other countries, European firms probably have less need for formal intercultural education than US or Japanese companies.

- *Japan.* Although Japanese firms invested extensively in Asia in the 1960s and 1970s, major direct investment in North America and Europe took off only in the mid-1980s, largely the result of rapid appreciation of the yen after 1985 (*endaka*). The success they have made of their investments is largely due to a keen understanding of local conditions and markets. In the US, for example, Japanese producers have often surprised US executives by learning US consumers' needs—and filling them—better than many US firms. In Europe, only tariffs have kept Japanese firms from duplicating their US activity. Recently, companies from other Asian nations, notably South Korea and Taiwan, have successfully followed Japan's lead.

    With their increasing foreign investment, Japanese companies are becoming active participants in foreign communities, a role whose demands go beyond merely understanding market conditions. With a shift of gravity away from corporate headquarters, Japanese MNCs must contend with such issues as centralization vs local autonomy, staffing abroad and adaptation of Japanese executives to foreign cultures (a process eased by the permeation of Western culture in Japan), as well as the far-more-sensitive issue of helping LNs adapt to Japanese corporate culture. Although Japanese executives, on the whole, seem to fail less frequently than their US counterparts at overseas assignments, Japanese human resources managers suggest this may, in part, reflect the stoicism of Japanese expatriates, who characteristically endure rather than complain about adjustment problems and, perhaps, are concerned that their future careers may not be furthered by voicing too many complaints.

There are several factors that may account for the success of Japanese companies outside their home markets. One key difference between many Japanese and US firms (and, to a lesser extent, European companies) is the length of overseas executive postings. Japanese managers usually stay at least three years—and often more than five years—in the US or Europe, but when US or European executives serve in Japan, it is typically for shorter periods.

Such differences are most striking at the top of the corporate ladder. Sony's founder and chairman, Akio Morita, spends half his time in New York, reflecting his view that the US market is vital to the company's continued success. Few, if any, CEOs of US or European MNCs live for months on end in Japan, year after year, despite the country's vast market potential, its importance and the many obstacles non-Japanese firms face in penetrating the Japanese market.

Another key difference is language. Although relatively few Westerners speak Japanese, most Japanese executives posted abroad speak English competently, and, in some cases, are conversant in another European language.

But despite the striking accomplishments of many Japanese companies in foreign markets, Japanese executives are often disinclined to take on overseas assignments. The reasons for this are diverse, but executives cite the relatively long time they must spend abroad or difficulties in bridging the cultural gap between Japan and the West. A 1990 poll by the opinion research unit of Japan's leading business newspaper, *Nihon Keizai Shimbun* (Japan Economic Journal), found that 50.4% of the 1,500 corporate workers surveyed in Tokyo would turn down a foreign assignment, because it would disrupt relationships with peers and perhaps damage their careers. Only 15% said they would accept an outside posting, while the remaining 34.6% expressed no opinion.

While in the past companies were able to attract Japanese managers to foreign jobs with the lure of overseas travel, that is no
longer the case. Today, more Japanese are affluent, travel frequently
abroad as tourists and thus no longer need to rely on their employers to show them the world.

Japanese companies are now beginning to make changes in their
expatriate policies to ensure that they will have a pool of executives
to staff their overseas subsidiaries. Some now offer executives a
richer mix of incentives to leave headquarters. These include higher
compensation and, upon the family's return to Japan, housing assistance and tutoring for children who have been educated abroad to
help them gain admission to highly competitive schools.

The Global Manager: Creating a Cultural Hybrid

National differences notwithstanding, companies based in North
America, Europe and Japan have adopted programs to develop highly
skilled and versatile international executives. These programs' essential characteristics are:

■ *Greater use of foreign subsidiaries as a source of executives to fill senior
corporate management ranks.* Companies want to eliminate the divide
between the elite home-country personnel, who previously had
preferential access to top posts, and the "second-class" cadre of
LNs. Many MNCs have already created "equal rights" policies for
foreign subsidiary employees, in which they are considered on the
same basis as home-country candidates for all available promotions.
At Coca-Cola, CEO Roberto C. Goizueta began his ascent of the corporate ladder in his native Cuba. Former IBM vice chairman Kaspar
Cassani, a Swiss national, began his climb in Europe. At Colgate-
Palmolive, former CEO Keith Crane, a New Zealander, joined the
company as a mail clerk in Auckland.

Legal restrictions in many countries on the use of expatriate labor
played a role in this trend, but it has since accelerated for a variety
of reasons. Even where it is legal to use an expatriate or TCN, political discretion may counsel the hiring of an LN. Furthermore, LNs
normally cost less than expatriates. The difference is even more
pronounced at higher levels because of savings on housing and
other expatriate incentives. Moreover, as management-educa-
tion programs become more common outside the US, the quality
and uniformity of this source of talent is improving. Locals also

have the advantages of useful business contacts and language skills. However, developing a mostly local managerial corps presents challenges of its own. The most important is integrating locals into a corporate culture that frequently clashes with foreign standards of propriety and decorum.

- *Emergence of TCNs as a cost-effective pool of new talent.* An intermediate option between expatriates and LNs is the third-country national. TCNs are expatriates from countries other than the one where the MNC is based, and they usually have worked for the company in their home countries in the past. Although TCNs may lack firsthand knowledge of the country of assignment, they have already adjusted to the corporate culture. Third-country managers are used frequently in regions that share a common language, e.g., Latin America and Chinese-speaking parts of Southeast Asia.

  A key advantage of TCNs is that they do not bear the home-office stamp. This can either serve strategic business goals or be a simple acknowledgment of broader political realities. For example, recognizing the depth of anti-US sentiment south of the border, one major US MNC habitually grooms Canadians for the top post in the company's Mexican subsidiary. TCNs may also be called in to handle a difficult restructuring. Many MNCs, including IBM and Philips, eschew the term "third-country national," preferring to think of TCNs as simply expatriates from a country other than "home." This is in line with the global management philosophy of not distinguishing between staff that bears the same citizenship as the company and staff from other countries.

- *Globalized succession planning.* To develop global executives of the future, many companies, including those as diverse as Colgate-Palmolive and NEC, are now sending high-potential junior executives abroad at an early age. In addition, as companies accord international service the status it deserves, senior executives are becoming more willing to accept important overseas assignments. Today, it is not unusual for a senior executive to fulfill an important role abroad, and then, when the assignment is completed, return to a higher position back at headquarters. Meanwhile, many MNCs, including NEC and IBM, have adopted programs to move promising executives—who are from countries other than the MNC's home base—through headquarters to give them a better sense of the company's direction. Thus, today's advanced companies frequently have employees moving in all directions at once—from headquarters out, from overseas in—all with an eye to developing international savvy and matching the best people with assignments abroad.

The Importance of Training

To cope with the mix of nationalities now common at most MNCs, top managements are emphasizing training, particularly with a cross-cultural or international component. With respect to expatriates, the aim is to secure a successful adjustment to a new post and to ease the pain of repatriation when a foreign assignment is completed. Experience demonstrates that good training programs can dramatically reduce a company's failure rate in this area. Given the high costs associated with an unsuccessful international assignment, such training will generally pay for itself many times over.

Comprehensive expatriate training programs typically encompass all or several of the following components (each is discussed in detail later in this report):

- *Predeparture orientation.* Most companies find predeparture training a worthwhile investment. Significantly, the focus is squarely on the personal side since the majority of unsuccessful expatriate experiences are the result of the spouse or family's inability to adjust. A comprehensive expatriate program must include assistance for the family, as well as the executive.

  To manage this phase of the training process, many MNCs use outside consultants who offer specialized predeparture training. Other corporations conduct this training themselves. However it is accomplished, such programs should stress the firsthand experience of former expatriates and the realities of day-to-day life, both practical and emotional: how to get a driver's license, which are the best schools and where to shop, as well as how to deal with homesickness and loneliness, how to make friends and meet with other expatriates and how to solve problems children may have in adapting. Language training for family members—who have to function on their own, without much staff or office support—is also critical.

- *Cultural "conditioning."* In addition to predeparture counseling, many firms offer other types of cross-cultural training. These differ from conventional executive training, because they stress cultural precepts that may run counter to traditional business behavior. Executives who work abroad may have to act in ways contrary to what they have learned from years of training and experience at home. For example, a Japanese manager who comes to the US may have to act assertively in certain situations, whereas that kind of behavior at home would run contrary to custom. Similarly, US executives who seek to do business in Japan must learn to be patient and deferential—two qualities that may actually hurt their careers back home.

- *Training in local business practices.* In addition to cross-cultural training, executives who work abroad may require additional instruction to put their functional and product expertise into an international context. Often they need to acquire a knowledge of local marketing methods, financial practices or technical standards. Courses range from the catchall "doing business in" variety, designed to appeal to executives of all nationalities, to courses tailored to specific problems, e.g., differences between Japanese and US hiring practices. Finally, because of differences in educational standards and resources from country to country, some employees, particularly those from developing economies, may require extensive management education to bring their knowledge and skills up to the company's expectations.

- *Language coaching.* Although all companies offer intensive language training to employees prior to foreign posting, not all companies consider language proficiency crucial to success in a foreign position. Japanese firms are known to stress language ability—at least the ability to speak English. Typically, European firms prefer a degree of language proficiency. US firms, on the whole, are less aggressive in stressing language training. However, the necessity to speak the local language will depend on the nature of the job. Marketing people, as a rule, must speak the local language, but technical people may get by with less proficiency. The need for language training also varies by business sector. In the highly global banking and financial sector, English has emerged as the lingua franca—and many executives already speak it—paradoxically reducing the need for company training. In contrast, manufacturing personnel are less likely to speak a foreign language and will require more language training in the event a company wishes to transfer technology overseas. Importantly, linguistic facility is often considered more crucial for TCNs and LNs than for expatriates.

- *Management training.* Besides offering simple courses in business practices, companies have begun to provide more involved programs in international management. Often reserved for upper-level executives, but occasionally presented to younger ones, such programs typically serve as prestigious rewards for outstanding global managers and important tools to help expand their knowledge. Larger companies may create and offer such courses themselves, but many firms make use of advanced management-training courses offered by the top international business schools.

- *On-the-job training.* Work experience is the best training program. The sequence and nature of executives' assignments will inevitably play a decisive role in their development. To identify talented individuals and then accelerate their progress through the company, most MNCs have devised a high-potential advancement program. Typically, high potentials receive advanced opportunities, challenges and introductions to senior executives from whom they stand to learn the most. It's equally important for the future success of the company to have senior managers meet high potentials in order to guide them forward in their careers.

Other Essentials: What Happens Before and After

Effective management development begins with successful recruitment and selection, which, in turn, originate with a thorough understanding of what makes a strong manager. In filling international assignments, judicious use of executive recruitment firms, together with a rigorous screening process, can help take the guesswork out of placement. The screening process for expatriate positions should also include interviews with candidates' families to ascertain their adaptability to a different culture.

After completion of an assignment, a successful repatriation is the key to harvesting the knowledge, skills and experience the executive has attained abroad. Planning for repatriation should begin well before an executive's assignment ends. One of the most important aspects of any return program is motivational adjustment. In many cases, the very qualities that ensure achievement in the field can cause friction at headquarters. This may occur when executives who have enjoyed decision-making autonomy overseas encounter the bureaucratic strictures imposed by their proximity to the corporate hierarchy.

The most critical part of constructive repatriation of managers is to find them appropriate positions at home. This has long been a key problem for MNCs and one that frequently costs companies the continued services of their seasoned returnees. The expectation of equitable treatment in a domestic job assignment upon return is as important to the success of a company's international management-development program as preparing executives properly to go abroad and making sure they have the tools to do a good job while there. Recognizing that selecting, supporting and repatriating an expatriate is an ongoing process, AT&T has fashioned a program that treats an executive assignment as one continuous cycle.

Global career-path planning, developmental assignments, moving executives from one foreign post to another before bringing them back to headquarters, the use of headquarters-based mentors while executives are overseas and after they are repatriated—all of these practices can provide executives with greater incentives to accept their first international assignments and to stay with the company after they return home. Such efforts enable companies to benefit fully from the abilities and knowledge expatriate executives obtain from their international assignments.

2

Executive Recruitment and Selection

Executive Summary

Recruiting and selecting managers for service at foreign affiliates are essential parts of any company's worldwide human resources program. For all but specialized positions, most MNCs interviewed prefer to fill international executive slots internally. To facilitate recruiting and promoting from within, more and more corporations are moving toward global personnel systems, which permit them to tap their worldwide managerial talent pool. When filling positions externally, MNCs hire directly and through executive recruiters. In either case—hiring from inside or outside—proper screening techniques play a critical role in identifying the best candidate for each international executive position that becomes available.

Good international management begins with hiring a talented crop of managers predisposed to international assignments. Although training, enlightened career pathing and other management-development techniques can help a company get the most from its managers, these techniques will work best on people who have an aptitude for international work. Hence, good recruiting can play an important role in developing a topflight international executive corps. Many factors must be considered in recruiting and selecting candidates for overseas positions. However, the first decision a company must make in filling a particular position is whether to recruit locally or abroad.

Basic Choices in Recruitment

Management has, essentially, three options in recruiting for an international executive position: (1) expatriates, (2) local nationals and (3) third-country nationals.

Although expatriates tend to dominate the early stages of a corporation's activities abroad, most MNCs prefer to use LNs whenever possible. One reason is that tax and compensation factors can make the employment costs for an expatriate (or a TCN, for that matter) prohibitive. Another is that governments, as a condition for doing business, may require the company to hire as many local citizens as possible. Finally, LNs are generally much better acquainted with the local market, government policies and business scene than are managers from other countries.

The number of LNs employed at MNC affiliates has increased markedly in recent years.

- *IBM*, for example, has approximately 3,000 employees who currently work outside their own countries. That figure represents less than 1% of the company's global work force of 373,000.

- *Bull*, the French electronics manufacturer, has only 300 of some 46,000 employees (0.6%) working outside their own countries. Such numbers are typical of most large non-Japanese MNCs.

Japanese MNCs

Japanese MNCs present a different picture, reflecting a tradition of ambivalence about the benefits of "going local," as well as their relatively recent status as large-scale overseas investors. As many large Japanese firms have progressed from exporters to true MNCs, they have retained a system that sends out many top executives from home. On the whole, the majority of Japanese MNCs still believes the extra expense and complexity of using expatriates is justified by their expertise, loyalty to headquarters and understanding of the corporate culture. At foreign subsidiaries, generally, expatriates are concentrated at higher levels, whereas local nationals dominate lower-level positions.

- *Matsushita Electric Industrial (MEI).* Officials at Osaka-based MEI admit that more than half of the directors in overseas affiliates are Japanese and that this tendency is especially conspicuous at relatively new overseas companies. Looking into the future, however, MEI officials affirm their company's commitment to increase the percentage of its foreign executives who are local nationals.

- *Fujitsu America Inc (FAI).* At FAI, based in San Jose, California, just over 120 of the 2,109 staff in July 1990 were Japanese expatriates on overseas assignment, a total of about 6%. The percentage has declined during the history of Tokyo-based Fujitsu Ltd's US holding company. "When I came here about seven years ago, it was as high as 10%," says John G. Klinestiver, FAI's vice president for human resources. Although the number of Japanese expatriates has held constant over this period, their percentage has declined as the firm has hired more US employees.

But some Japanese firms have advanced further in this process of localization than others.

- *NEC,* for example, has only an estimated 800 Japanese expatriates out of a work force of 39,000. "The proportion of our work force that is locally hired is rising every year," says Hajime Hasegawa, senior vice president and director of the NEC Institute of Management in Tokyo. Similarly, Tokyo-based *Fuji Xerox* has only about 130 expatriates out of over 13,700 employees.

Local Nationals

There are several reasons why the use of LNs is gaining in popularity.

- *Reduced cost.* Even in countries where qualified executives are in short supply, LNs typically enjoy a cost advantage resulting from savings in relocation costs, salary premiums and housing, school and other overseas allowances. In addition, LNs require no predeparture training.

  Bibiana Santiago, *AT&T*'s human resources director for Europe, the Middle East and Africa, estimates that the cost of maintaining an expatriate can be as much as three to four times the executive's stay-at-home salary. The exact figure depends on such factors as family size, location and length of an assignment. The latter can be particularly important, because the cost of a move must be amortized over the length of the posting.

Henri C. Debuisser, executive director of personnel, organization and corporate affairs at *Rank Xerox*, points out that the cost of maintaining a senior-level expatriate is particularly high.

- *LNs help smooth relations with governments.* In most countries today, governments insist that LNs fill all jobs except when no qualified local national can be found. For example, the US Immigration and Naturalization Service (INS) discourages the use of expatriates for technical, professional and management positions at the US subsidiaries of non-US companies unless those companies can show that expatriates are essential to the operation of the business.

  Volvo AB contends that an INS application alone impedes the relocation of executives, since it requires the intervention of a US immigration lawyer to expedite the processing of work permits and visa applications. This commonly takes several months.

  Countries may have other rules that favor the use of LNs. For example, Germany requires that all meetings of corporate boards of directors be conducted in German. So if a company's top managers—and members of the board—are not German, they must at least speak the language. Although there is no formal requirement to this effect in Italy, it is customary for board meetings to be conducted in Italian. Canada requires that a majority of board members of federally incorporated companies be Canadian citizens.

  It is widely acknowledged that Switzerland is especially restrictive vis-à-vis expatriates. *Rank Xerox's* experience there is fairly typical. "Switzerland," says Debuisser, "has very tight rules regarding labor permits....You've literally got to prove that only this individual has the skills to prevent the company from going bankrupt."

  Philips increasingly prefers that LNs run its country operations, even where regulations that require use of locals are lax. "For instance, our general manager in Taiwan is Taiwanese, our general manager in Italy is Italian, our general manager in the US is American and our general manager in Switzerland is Swiss," says managing director of the corporate staff bureau J. D. de Leeuw.

- *Cultural bonding.* LNs have a special advantage: They share a set of common cultural, linguistic and religious antecedents with their fellow employees. This is particularly important in developing countries, where an expatriate is often seen as a tool of a former colonial power. Many companies therefore put LNs in the most visible positions, such as sales and marketing, because they speak the language and share a common background.

IBM's director of executive resources and development, Don Laidlaw, says, "The people at IBM Japan in marketing are Japanese. Our marketers in France are French."

France's *Bull* takes a similar position. "We want to be local in each country," says a senior manager. "We want to be near our customers, speak the language of our customers and have a good understanding of our customers."

- *Philips'* de Leeuw agrees: "A local national in a locally oriented job, like a sales job, knows the culture much better and is in a much better position to operate," he says.

Expatriates

In light of the conditions that favor LNs, why should an MNC use expatriates at all? The companies interviewed for this report say expatriates are used (1) to provide the high level of technical or functional knowledge and experience that is required for a particular position; (2) to provide a promising executive with international experience; or (3) to transmit clearly the corporate image or a degree of home-office concern. In the latter case, the expatriate does not necessarily have to be a senior executive to convey a sense of corporate authority. Indeed, even a relatively junior employee who shares the nationality of the home company may be perceived as a representative of headquarters—although this situation may create some strain if locals believe the junior executive lacks commensurate experience.

Illustrating this third case, in which an expatriate may be used to convey corporate authority, *AT&T*'s Santiago recalls that she once considered sending a TCN to a European subsidiary: "I remember asking a local manager whether I would be supporting him if I hired another European executive to help with a certain project. He said, `No. Why would I want another European telling me what to do? If someone from headquarters tells me what to do, I can accept it because the person represents the corporate perspective.'" LN managers are more willing to take direction from expatriates than TCNs, because the person from the company's home country "brings something that someone else can't bring," she says.

Although more and more MNCs have begun elevating LNs to top management positions, most senior positions are still occupied by expatriates. For example, at *Fujitsu America*, most expatriates are second- or third-level managers who have various US citizens reporting to them. Besides occupying top management slots, expatriates also staff many manufacturing and engineering positions. In a 1989 survey of expatriates of 56 US companies, the consulting firm Moran, Stahl & Boyer (MS&B) found that 54% of expatriates occupied managerial positions while 31% occupied technical roles.

Whatever the reason for using an expatriate, a company usually has to persuade the host-country authorities that the expatriate possesses skills or attributes that are not available locally.

- *JVs and acquisitions.* Some companies find that several rationales for using expatriates come into play when the objective is to start an over-seas joint venture (JV) or manage either a JV or a recent acquisition. A company that embarks on either operation is unlikely to have its own human resources operation in place locally, and, in most cases, it must use the work force of the JV partner or the acquired firm.

  Particularly in the early days of a JV or takeover, the foreign-based MNC will need people thoroughly familiar with its business, who have specific management or technical abilities and are able to look out for its interests. Expatriates are also valued for the feedback they can provide headquarters regarding the partner's or acquisition's strengths and weaknesses and for the influence they can wield over key business decisions. Later on, expatriates may still be needed to supervise technology transfers and implement systems from home.

  However, to conform to local laws, which may well make hiring the largest possible number of LNs a condition of doing business, companies have to make a very strong case for bringing in expatri-ates. Indeed, the extent of involvement of a JV's foreign partner in senior management and the amount of technology transfer and training the foreign partner provides may be "bartered" for tax relief, loan guarantees and other investment incentives.

  Although *Fuji Xerox* uses local management at most of its JVs, top management will typically maintain at least one expatriate there at a high level, such as executive vice president. Normally, says Masahiro Haraguchi, deputy manager of the firm's management and resource development center, the Japanese assignee chosen must have a thorough understanding of "Fuji Xerox's general man-agement principles" and also be able to understand the local culture.

- *Midlevel managers.* MNCs also fill midlevel and even junior posi-tions abroad with expatriates, in some cases because they possess essential skills, but also because these are high-potential employees being groomed for bigger things. (High potentials are discussed in detail in Chapter 5.) Such postings are often called development assignments, but even in these cases (where the purpose is to provide special training), the individual must possess some unique qualities to satisfy legal requirements.

Third-Country Nationals

The third option for management is use of TCNs, known in some companies as "cross posters" or international assignees. They are simply expatriates from a country other than the one where an MNC is based.

Traditionally, TCNs have been the "hired guns" of international personnel. Often brought in to carry out layoffs, restructurings or

---

NCR Taiwan: Choosing Between Expatriates and Local Nationals

It is the policy of NCR Taiwan to use LNs whenever possible. A tight local labor market, however, means that NCR Taiwan, like other firms on the island, must turn to expatriates employed in other NCR subsidiaries more often than it might otherwise choose. "It is hard to find local people for just about every position," says David Wang, manager of personnel resources. "If we hire a new local, by recruiting locally or using a local headhunter, he will have to learn the NCR system. If we hire an expat who doesn't have to learn the NCR system, he will have to adjust to the local environment. So we have to judge which alternative is better for the particular case."

The type of employee the company hires typically depends on the job. "If we want to hire a marketing specialist, a local person may be better because he would know Taiwan's business environment," says Wang. "But if we need to fill a technical function, we may have to choose an expat, as knowledge of NCR's products and the company's system will be more critical for that job." At present, out of the eight executives who report to the country manager, two are expatriates—one in finance, the other in engineering—and the other six are LNs.

The level and kind of position help determine whether to hire locally or to bring over an expatriate. Generally, says Wang, "the higher the position, the more things a local hire would have to learn about the company, and, thus, the greater the risk of failure." LNs who accept positions of responsibility must learn "a lot that is new to them about the company's operations, new subordinates, new colleagues and a new boss."

other difficult tasks, TCNs have acquired a reputation, particularly among LNs, of being a floating class of executives not linked to any one market and owing no particular allegiance to anyone in the company. It is precisely this freedom, however, that makes the TCN a great asset to headquarters. Having no identification with the home office or home country, a TCN is often ideally suited to supervise a restructuring and can help redirect what might otherwise be nationalistic sentiment against the parent company.

Expanding the Role of TCNs. Nevertheless, the role of TCNs is being expanded beyond "putting out fires." Many now serve as coordinators of a firm's long-term regional market strategy. Particularly in regions where the same language is spoken, e.g., Latin America, TCNs are valuable alternatives to LNs. Not only do they speak the language and possess an intimate knowledge of local conditions, they have already made the adjustment to the corporate culture and can pursue strategic goals without bias. TCNs also expand the available labor pool—a major plus in markets plagued by shortages of seasoned managers.

Two prime areas for TCNs are Latin America and Asia. In a typical scenario, an MNC has its Latin American regional headquarters in, say, Mexico. Most probably, Mexico is the site of the firm's oldest or largest Latin American operation and has a strong local organization and considerable country and regional expertise. Therefore, when expanding into other Latin American markets, the parent company would be much more inclined to staff the new operation with executives from Mexico—either Mexicans or people from elsewhere in Latin America who have been working in Mexico—than from its home country.

Sometimes, the source of intraregional TCNs is simply a country operating unit rather than a regional headquarters. For example, *Coca-Cola*—with a large percentage of expatriate managers who are not US citizens—has deployed Chileans to management posts in other Spanish-speaking countries in Latin America. "We have four or five relatively young Chileans managing significant pieces of geography in Latin America," says D. Larry Kroh, Coca-Cola's director of human resources development.

Similarly, companies use ethnic Chinese TCNs in Asian economies where Chinese is widely spoken, including Hong Kong, China, Malaysia, Singapore and Taiwan. For instance, in the rush to develop business in China a few years ago, following that nation's economic liberalization, many MNCs hired executives from Hong Kong to spearhead their efforts, especially in Cantonese-speaking Guangdong province in southern China. In general, if a company has a particularly strong operation in one country, it often elects to use people of that nationality when it expands elsewhere.

Using TCNs in regions that share a common language provides yet another advantage. TCNs greatly expand the pool of candidates for significant positions in each country to include, theoretically, everyone with the proper background who speaks the language. This means that a country subsidiary's management can simply choose, to the extent permitted by the parent company's personnel system, the candidates with the best qualifications, no matter where they are located.

'Assignees'—Not TCNs.   Although the use of TCNs is increasing, the term *TCN* may be on its way out. In truly global companies, such as *IBM*, the concept is becoming outmoded. IBM does not speak of TCNs, but of *assignees*—international employees transferred from one country to another. Under the IBM system, a non-US national assigned abroad is the same as a US national assigned abroad. Although the company prefers to use LNs whenever possible, it scours the world to find the best-qualified individual when certain skills are unavailable in the market in which they are needed.

According to Peter J. Cohen, director of human resources and administrative services for *Dow Chemical Japan*, "you should simply choose the best person for the job," given availability, the candidate's ability to adapt overseas and the company's particular human resource development needs. One half of Dow Chemical Japan's expatriates are TCNs. Cohen, an Australian national himself, points out that by shifting local nationals abroad, a company can offer them an international perspective that enhances their potential value. "It's fairly natural," he explains. "If people live and work outside their own country, they learn about all sorts of new strategies and successful business practices that may be valuable back in their own country."

Toward a Global Pool of Management Talent

Identifying the people who are qualified to work overseas is a prerequisite for effective international recruitment and selection. If a company cannot readily recognize the most qualified candidates for an overseas assignment, it is unlikely to ultimately choose the best man or woman for the job. As a result, a growing number of firms, led by global giants IBM and Philips, have developed (or are working toward developing) systems that can identify talented executives throughout the world, ideally at early stages of their careers. Even if a company does not attempt to track "international" potential per se, it is well advised to develop a global system of personnel tracking to identify the best candidates for a job, wherever they may be. Thus, although IBM does not specifically monitor the international potential of its executives, it does keep track of promising executives throughout the world. (IBM's state-of-the-art personnel tracking program is described in Chapter 5.)

Matsushita, similarly, has begun to track personnel on a global basis. "We are now laying the groundwork for the future development of a global personnel system for top executives—vice presidents and above in US terms," says Nobuo Umeoka, assistant general manager of MEI's corporate personnel department. Matsushita's Osaka-based global headquarters hopes to finish the groundwork for the system by 1993.

Global selection systems enable a company to find the best person anywhere in the world for a given position in a short time—or, just as important, to discover that no one in the company has the right qualifications. Even if the firm ends up recruiting for the position externally, it can do so confidently, knowing that it has not overlooked a qualified internal candidate. To handle executive assessment, some firms use specialized assessment centers where managers undergo a battery of tests; others follow a less centralized approach. Where employees are assessed is not so important as that assessments are performed. Systematic assessment is the first step toward establishing overall strategic control over global management development.

**Finding Those Most Likely
to Succeed**

Colgate-Palmolive is already able to tap into a worldwide pool of executive talent. The company employs a centralized committee that consists of the chief operating officer, the division presidents, the head of global business development and a representative of human resources. Using a new corporate data bank, as well as firsthand knowledge, the company prepares a list of potential candidates for each significant international assignment. This list encompasses employees at headquarters and all other locations.

At the junior-executive level, *NCR*'s wholly owned subsidiary in Taiwan uses a consultant service to aid in career-pathing decisions. The company hired Personnel Development Inc (PDI), a Cambridge,

Massachusetts-based company that specializes in management assessment. After identifying young staffers who may have management potential, NCR sends them through a day-and-a-half PDI assessment program.

"In this program, everyone takes aptitude and personality tests and participates in an in-basket exercise," says NCR's Wang. In the in-basket exercise, employees are given a basketful of incoming documents. "Numerous documents, memos and communications are placed in the basket, and you have to put your comments on them—positive or negative—and make decisions about how to deal with them." PDI analyzes the results to identify the employee's development needs and potential strengths and weaknesses. NCR Taiwan then uses the report to help plan the individual's career path.

For its part, *NEC* pinpoints talent in its system by performing a subjective evaluation of all executives every three years, specifically on their "ability to adapt to international environments," says Masaru Yamamoto, general manager of the international education division of the NEC Institute of Management.

MEI also maintains a personnel data bank in its home office, with information on over 2,000 staff members who belong to what MEI calls the "international function." This category, which cuts across different disciplines, such as accounting, personnel and purchasing, enables the company to keep track of people best qualified for international assignments. Requirements include "foreign language capability and knowledge about other countries," says MEI's Umeoka.

The company also utilizes a "challenge" system to assess employee desires and abilities. "Every year we distribute a form to every employee in the corporation—now about 83,000 people," says Umeoka. "On this form, they tell us what they would like to do as a challenge for future assignments. This year, we added a new column where employees can indicate their desire to work in the international area. The data are stored in our computer and registered as an international data bank for our employees who are willing to work outside Japan." MEI intends to intensify its already extensive educational and training efforts to further develop the potential of these employees, particularly those who are involved in manufacturing activities.

Further up the line, the assessment of talent typically becomes the joint responsibility of a company's corporate human resources department and its line management. To keep track of performance, Sweden's *Atlas Copco* depends on the line manager and, at higher levels, the director with regional responsibility. Consider the case of a particular manager, say, someone who works in the firm's compressor business in Spain and is very capable. The president of the Sweden-based compressor division might develop a particular interest in this manager. Because presidents of divisions "are responsible for their own business, they have a very heavy say on people matters," says Bo Eklöf, the company's administrative director. "So the president of the compressor division would follow that Spanish manager's progress closely and would report to us informally that he is developing well and could be of great future use to the compressor group."

Another interesting approach to assessing international aptitude is the Overseas Assignment Inventory (OAI) system, developed by MS&B and used by *General Electric* (GE), among others (see figure on p. 33). Based on a standardized questionnaire, this system measures applicants according to a group of 12 character attributes. Results are then tabulated and graphed in the form of an OAI profile, which can reveal a great deal about an individual's international potential. These 12 categories are motivations, expectations, open-mindedness, respect for other beliefs, trust in people, tolerance, personal control, flexibility, patience, social adaptability, initiative, risk taking, sense of humor, interpersonal interest and spouse communication—all of which are valuable assets for an expatriate to possess. The graph on the following page depicts how these results can then be analyzed. The line represents the individual's score on each of the 12 attributes, whereas the broad band represents the average as derived from thousands of other responses. By comparing the individual's ratings with the average, it is possible to identify a job candidate's strengths and weaknesses.

Evaluating a Candidate's `Intangibles'

Although it remains difficult to predict who will do well in a foreign environment, previous success overseas often provides a valuable clue to future performance abroad. Companies often carefully examine managers' performances in limited international situations as indicators of how they might perform in larger overseas assignments.

Beyond superior technical and managerial skills, an effective international executive displays a combination of desirable personal qualities. These include adaptability, independence, leadership—even charisma.

- *Ethnicity/language.* For many companies, it is important that expatriates and TCNs have ethnic or other connections to the assigned

Overseas Assignment Inventory Profile

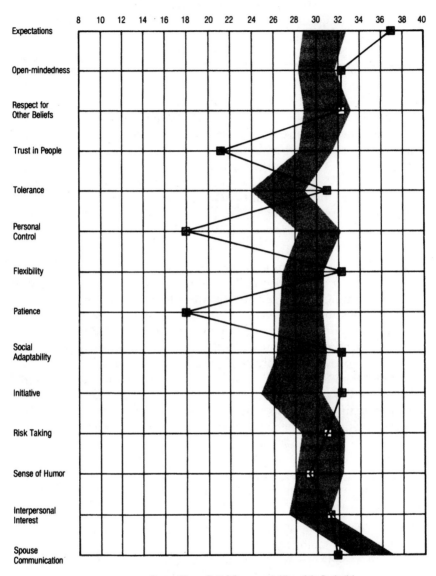

Source: Moran, Stahl & Boyer, a subsidiary of the Prudential

area. For example, when *AT&T* staffed its joint venture with the Spanish company Telefonica, "the core management team we had in Spain were all Hispanic Americans," says human resources director Santiago. "We all spoke the language and, essentially, had similar cultural roots."

Similarly, *NCR Taiwan*'s two expatriates are ethnic Chinese from Malaysia and the Philippines. "Because this is a marketing and service company, the expats are all overseas Chinese. Even if they can't write or read Chinese fluently, they can understand spoken Chinese and speak it," says NCR's Wang. In turn, when NCR Taiwan sends an employee abroad, for example, to global corporate headquarters in Dayton, Ohio, the subsidiary puts a high priority on the person's ability to speak English.

One of the key criteria in the computer profiles of Coca-Cola's managers is linguistic ability. This enables the company, when it begins to search for someone to fill an executive position at one of its overseas units, to quickly spot those who speak more than one language.

- *Cultural fit.* Apart from language skills and ethnicity, other factors may affect an executive's ability to perform well in a new cultural environment. Cultural sensitivity and interest in the foreign culture can help ensure an expatriate's success. In turn, an executive's personality will often determine how he or she is received by locals.

  Dow Chemical Japan, for example, has found that seasoned executives have proven far more successful in the Japanese business environment than their more junior counterparts. "With rare exceptions, this is not the place to bring a young hotshot to take on a middle-to-senior management job," notes Dow's Cohen. "We might give a younger staffer a specialist role, but not a leadership position." Generally, Dow prefers its executives in Tokyo to have had some prior international experience, given the value placed on seniority by Japanese businessmen and the subtleties of conducting business in Japan, not to mention the cultural gap between Japanese and American society.

- *Family life.* When its managers go to the US, *NCR Taiwan* also attempts, via a management-assessment service provided by PDI, to identify executives who are open minded. NCR Taiwan's Wang looks for "people who can learn new things, are flexible and outgoing and who have a happy family background."

  Most firms would agree with Wang—a stable personal and family life is very important to a successful expatriate assignment.

Hence, most companies screen potential executives' families, although the extent of the "investigation" varies. Most interview employees and their families, but do so in a nonconfrontational way, leaving it up to the family to raise potential problems. Typically, the atmosphere is that of a forum for open discussion. The stability of the candidate's marriage is especially significant. As Wang of NCR says, "If a manager has a good relationship with his wife, going overseas can bring the couple closer and make their marriage more successful." However, if the couple already has conflicts and the executive cannot count on the support of his wife, a foreign assignment can, says Wang, "break the family."

- *Personal problems.* Checking into employees' private lives is a very sensitive issue. A company normally gains some insight into its employees' characters and habits over the course of their employment—anyone with obvious problems would not be considered for an overseas assignment in the first place. Barring anything obvious, it is up to the interviewer to spot signs of trouble. "If there is a problem, there's no sense in transporting that 2,000 miles," notes one human resources professional. Thus, interviewers may try in subtle ways to find out if someone has certain problems that could spell trouble later on, such as alcoholism.

- *Marital status.* Most people sent abroad are married and male (see box on pp. 36–37 for a discussion of women who work abroad). Generally, firms have found that it is easier for a married expatriate to adapt to a foreign environment than for a single person. *Acer Inc,* the Taiwan-based producer of computers, for example, prefers to post older, married men to its larger international affiliates. "But in smaller operations," says John Wang, Acer's senior vice president for corporate administration, "where we only have two or three people, then singles are okay."

  NEC takes a somewhat different view. Masaru Yamamoto notes that "at smaller or new offices where our executives may have to attend more social functions, it may be helpful if an assignee is married. On social occasions, such as dinner parties where couples normally come together, attendance by a married couple would be preferable to suit Western customs." However, he points out that, often, spouses of Japanese expatriates stay in Japan to care for the educational needs of their children.

Rank Xerox, too, has observed that executives may benefit from the stability of marriage. The company does not keep computer records of married employees, because in some countries this may

Recruiting Women
for International Posts

Many observers agree that women have made good progress in climbing the corporate ladder in recent years. Success has been particularly marked in the US, but women have made important strides in other countries as well. Nevertheless, women remain less likely than men to be offered international assignments or to seek them out. Despite the occasional success story of a woman who gains acceptance in spite of cultural norms, acceptance of female executives remains problematic in many parts of the world. In some countries, it is virtually impossible, no matter what a company's intentions.

Problems can go beyond the cultural to the legal. For example, says *AT&T's* Santiago, herself an expatriate from the US stationed in Brussels, it can be difficult for a woman even to get through immigration in some Arab states. In Saudi Arabia, a woman would have to be prepared to wear traditional dress and, on certain occasions, a veil. (Other Arab nations, e.g., Bahrain, other Gulf states and Egypt, have proven more amenable to women executives.)

Santiago says the US is the most advanced country in terms of providing women with opportunities. In contrast, she says Europe is less progressive, though "throughout Europe, I would say that we're making some tremendous strides." Some Asian countries, such as Hong Kong and Singapore, have begun to promote more women to higher positions. Japan, however, remains an area where women have made relatively few advances. However, even Japanese firms, in recent years, have begun attempts to redress this imbalance.

At *Fuji Xerox*, for example, five women have reached the level of section manager throughout the entire company. To further promote the advancement of female employees, "we first began sending women for overseas training in the US just four years ago," says Fuji Xerox's Haraguchi. Of the five young staffers sent for overseas training each year (see Chapter 5, "Programs for High Potentials"), "we do our best to include at least one woman," says Haraguchi. He adds that "in spite of the equal opportunity law that came into effect in Japan in 1986, there are still laws on the books [concerning restrictions on women working at night and so forth] which complicate matters."

Although some Japanese firms claim to have begun hiring more female executives recently, few women can yet be found in high-level positions. Masaru Yamamoto, general manager of the international education division of the NEC Institute of Management, says that *NEC* has some female executives "but as yet they do not have the level of experience of senior executives."

Retaining Women as Well as Recruiting Them

A key element in promoting more women into the management ranks, both domestically and overseas, is to provide for their needs once they have been hired. According to AT&T's Santiago, support networks in the US make it easier to prosper there than elsewhere. In Europe, "we don't have as proactive or progressive programs," she says. "We're on the upswing, but we have yet to formalize support as we do in the US. There is one issue of recruiting women, and there's another one of retaining them. And if you don't have the supportive structure and aren't able to retain them, then that's almost as bad as not attracting them in the first place."

Being a female expatriate, however, can have its advantages, compared with being simply a local businesswoman. "You can sometimes get on better if you're viewed as a expat woman, because there's a perception that you're a `corporate' person, you represent the company," says Santiago.

One way to enhance conditions for female executives may be to provide increased flexibility in working hours. *Philips,* for example, offers maternity leave and contemplates adding flexibility in daily working hours.

To retain female expatriates, companies often must hire spouses or facilitate their hiring at other companies. Accommodating dual-career marriages is a problem in any case, but particularly when sending a female executive overseas, since few men are, as of yet, willing to interrupt their careers. Although many companies point to measures to facilitate dual-career marriages in the future, this may be easier said than done. For example, Peter J. Cohen of *Dow Chemical Japan* observes that, at least in Asia, "few MNCs are large enough to absorb an expatriate spouse as well as an executive. Some companies might have this capability in Japan, but many only have a few expatriate positions." Thus, even if expatriates' spouses worked for the same company, the Japanese subsidiary would have a hard time finding them a position.

The Future

Although female expats remain a small minority of total expatriates, that may change in the future. "When you look at all the demographic trends, analysts predict a shortage of qualified graduates and managerial talent in the future," says Philips' J. D. de Leeuw. "With women making up 50% of the total work force, they are, of course, a very interesting potential group of managers. I think that we are definitely going to pay much more attention to getting females into more senior positions. That is already a normal element, for instance, in the US or some countries in the Far East."

be considered discriminatory. Marital status can come into play, however, if the company is sending an employee on a difficult assignment to a country where a spouse and children might be at risk. Rank Xerox has found family stability to be a factor in expatriate success, particularly for executives placed in difficult environments, in the Third World, for instance. Conversely, the firm has found that when an executive's marriage breaks apart, he or she is likely to begin experiencing major problems at work as well.

In the case of married couples, *Dow Chemical Japan*'s Cohen points out that the difficulty of finding a job for a spouse in Japan argues in favor of hiring an expatriate whose partner is willing to forgo work for an extended period of time. Whether work is available depends on the spouse's profession. "It's not going to be easy here if we're talking about lawyers or nurses. Teachers may have a better chance."

- *Health.* Most companies perform medical screenings of potential international assignees, and some check a candidate's family as well. In general, companies want to know if there are any health problems that would force them to spend thousands of extra dollars after sending someone out into the field. GE's government electric systems division, which sends teams of expatriates on relatively short-term projects, is typical of many firms in subjecting candidates to an intensive medical exam. The company looks for potentially severe problems that could require the executive to return home and also ensures that good treatment is available locally for chronic, but manageable, conditions.

Recruiting: Inside or Outside?

In their home countries, most companies prefer to recruit executives for international jobs internally through promotion and transfers. In addition, firms that have international trainee programs for new business-school graduates do on-campus recruiting. Overseas, MNCs often have to look outside to a greater extent, because the company's employee pool is smaller, management-development systems are generally less advanced and campus recruiting is less active. If the company is primarily a sales organization, external recruitment may also make more sense, because knowledge of the market may outweigh that of corporate policies, technology or style of business. In the case of a start-up, external hiring (for staff other than a core of expatriates) is often the only practical option.

- *Philips* meets most of its management needs internally, both at headquarters and overseas. However, it makes an exception when it comes to sales or marketing personnel abroad. "We tend to recruit from the inside for key positions, such as business unit managers in a product division, because these people need extensive international experience with *this* company to function effectively," says Philips' de Leeuw. "But if we need a marketing or sales executive in the US or Taiwan, for example, we could also recruit from the outside." The company sticks to headhunters with strong international capabilities. "Our main criteria are reliability and an excellent reputation internationally," he adds.

- *Rank Xerox* normally keeps internal candidates in mind for any openings, but from time to time it may experience a "hiccup" in the system. For example, it may need to fill several senior positions simultaneously. According to Rank Xerox's Debuisser, management decided about four years ago to go outside more often than before to "bring new blood into the company. It's all a question of balance," he says.

- *IBM* today recruits almost entirely from its own ranks. "Our practice is to hire people and develop them within their organizations in each of our countries," says IBM's Laidlaw. "Twenty-five to 35 years ago, when we set up some of these country organizations, we brought in some people at the higher levels because we were just getting started." Today, however, it's rare for an IBM executive to be hired from outside.

- *Colgate-Palmolive* recently began recruiting more externally. Although still committed to promoting from within, the company believes "it's healthy to have a mix of newcomers and longtime employees, so we gain the benefit of management skills we may not have grown in-house yet," says director of management and organizational development R. Alicia Whitaker. The company looks for a recruiter with a global network of offices. "There are also smaller recruiting firms that may have intense industry expertise or functional expertise or a very strong network in a particular part of the world that we're interested in," she says. Whatever firm is selected, the company sees clarifying the specifications as "the most critical part of the entire search."

- *NCR Taiwan* utilizes headhunters only for finding high-level personnel in Taiwan's tight labor market. In the past, the firm tried advertising, but this method proved ineffective: "If someone is performing very well at his present job, he will not respond to your ad," says

Staffing for Short-Term Assignments Abroad

There are some significant differences between the recruitment and selection processes used for standard postings overseas (say, two to five or more years) and those for shorter project-oriented assignments that last less than a year.

One large MNC that does a great deal of short-term work for foreign clients, including governments, is often required to create a team of expatriates virtually from scratch.

In 1990, a foreign government solicited bids for a firm to provide support services in the development of a complex technology installation. As part of the deal, the firm was required to select 12 engineers to go in country to serve as engineering and design consultants. As a first step in selecting these 12, the company posted the jobs internally. Of 76 applicants, all but 26 were eliminated on technical grounds. The remainder then went through a screening process, "which included a spouse interview, a family interview, medical exams, discussion of the firm's compensation policies and relocation procedures and, finally, a police and reference check," says the manager in charge.

To help assess the candidates' adaptability to the overseas location, the firm used various screening systems and assessed individuals by discussing such qualitative issues as "how frustrated they get traveling or waiting in line and the fact that they're not going to have the same standard of living."

Finally, the company selected 14 candidates—12 plus two alternates as a "safety margin" to cover natural attrition. Of those selected, only one had actual international experience. This very small proportion is not unusual in the case of technically oriented short-term assignments.

NCR's Wang. To meet its needs for local managers, the Taipei-based firm uses recruiters who specialize in different management functions. Once it becomes clear that a position cannot be filled from available local resources, Wang can search for an expatriate from within NCR's ranks by going through the NCR Pacific Group office in Dayton or by utilizing its own contacts with other NCR subsidiaries. Decisions to hold interviews or extend offers to prospec-

~ tive candidates are made only after mutual agreement is reached between the relevant NCR offices. "After the local management has decided to extend an offer, we still have to notify the Pacific Group office to expedite the administrative procedures for expatriate assignments. There is no way that an exit assignment can be made without the approval of local management," Wang emphasizes.

- At *Dow Chemical Japan,* almost all non-Japanese executives were developed within the firm. "Virtually all our international executives are transfers from within the company," says Cohen, although Dow Chemical's Hong Kong subsidiary has hired some local staff through headhunters.

While many US and European firms prefer to hire at the university level and develop talent internally, Japanese companies are even stronger believers in cultivating young talent, often for careers as generalists. The Japanese practice of lifetime employment stresses step-by-step development of internal personnel in many functional areas. Most firms have a long tradition of recruiting directly from Japanese universities. In their overseas operations, however, Japanese MNCs are more willing to look outside, using headhunters and other means. Firms that are in the process of rapidly expanding overseas may have no choice but to recruit externally.

- *Matsushita Electric Corp of America* often recruits externally in the US by placing ads or relying on the services of executive recruiters. The company has also hired directly from US campuses, replicating its practice in Japan. "It's very rare for us to recruit outside executives in Japan," says Matsushita's Umeoka.

- *NEC* hires 90–95% of its new recruits directly from Japanese universities. "But outside Japan," says NEC Institute of Management's Yamamoto, "the situation is very different." In some cases, NEC uses headhunters; in others, it buys ads in local newspapers. A recruiting firm offers the advantage of narrowing the list of candidates. "When we use public media, like newspapers, we find that it's often impossible for us to make a short list quickly from the large number of applicants we get," he says. "However, professional recruiters screen people to a point where we can judge from a short list. This way is much more efficient." Apart from cost, Yamamoto believes the only real downside of using recruiters is that they sometimes fail to produce suitable candidates.

- *Fuji Xerox* is unusual among Japanese firms in its practice of recruiting more actively away from university campuses. Established in 1962, the joint venture between Xerox and Fuji is a relatively young

Global Search Firms: The Top 10*

Rank	Name/Address/Contact	1989 Billings			Number of Professionals		Offices	
		World	US	Non-US	Recruiters	Researchers	US	Non-US
1	Korn/Ferry Int'l 1800 Century Park East, Ste 900 Los Angeles, CA 90067 (213) 879-1834 Richard M. Ferry, President	103.3	65.9	37.4	259	86	17	25
2	Russell Reynolds Associates 200 Park Avenue New York, NY 10166 (212) 351-2000 Hobson Brown, Jr., President	87.0	53.5	33.5	196	44	12	10
3	Spencer Stuart & Associates 55 East 52nd Street New York, NY 10055 (212) 407-0200 Robert Benson, Managing Director	75.0	35.0	40.0	150	104	9	22
4	Egon Zehnder Int'l 55 East 59th Street New York, NY 10022 (212) 838-9199 A. Daniel Meiland, Regional Director/ North America	73.0	8.2	64.8	145		4	30
5	Heidrick & Struggles 125 South Wacker Drive Chicago, IL 60606 (312) 372-8811 Charles Ratigan, Managing Partner	57.4	37.3	20.1	147	105	13	11

6	Ward Howell Int'l Inc 99 Park Avenue New York, NY 10016 (212) 697-3730	45.3	12.6	32.5	118	57	11	24
7	Nordeman Grimm Inc 717 Fifth Avenue New York, NY 10022 (212) 935-1000 Jacques C. Nordeman, Chairman	30.5	5.5	25.0	15	7	2	12
8	Boyden Int'l Inc 260 Madison Avenue New York, NY 10016 (212) 685-3400 Malcolm MacGregor, President	30.2	12.5	17.8	95	57	10	30
9	Paul Ray & Carre Orban 301 Commerce Street, Ste 2300 Fort Worth, TX 76102 (817) 334-0500 Paul R. Ray, Jr., President & CEO	27.5	14.4	13.1	73	58	8	12
10	Norman Broadbent Int'l 65 Curzon Street London, UK W1Y 7PE (071) 629-9626 Bruce J. Robertson, Managing Director	25.8	3.4	22.4	46	18	2	8

*SOURCE: *Executive Recruiter News*, Kennedy Publications.

firm in Japan and has not yet developed the strong university recruiting tradition and networks enjoyed by older Japanese companies. "Last year, we recruited about 500 university graduates, but brought in 300 midcareer hires and 20 management-level hires from outside," says Fuji Xerox's Haraguchi.

Corporate Involvement in Overseas Hiring

In general, most foreign staffing is managed by the offshore subsidiaries, with little or no input from headquarters. However, for the most senior positions, particularly those that may be filled by expatriates, the home office is more likely to become involved. When it *is* involved in hiring, headquarters usually has the final say.

According to Wang, NCR is an exception: Corporate headquarters in Dayton, Ohio, gives country managers the final say. Within the local subsidiary, line management and personnel share responsibility for assignments. "Each hiring decision is mutually made by the line manager and personnel manager," he says. "They have the right to say yes, but I reserve the right to say no."

Says *Coca-Cola's* Kroh, "Each foreign subsidiary is responsible for its own hiring. The identification and the ultimate selection is made by the local group with our input and assistance, but it's very definitely the responsibility of the hiring manager to make the final selection."

For *NEC*, the division of responsibility for hiring decisions differs in Japan and overseas. In Japan, line management and personnel cooperate on staffing assignments, but personnel retains veto power. Outside Japan, the general manager and the personnel department also work together. The final choice is made by the line manager, rather than the personnel manager.

At *Dow Chemical Japan*, line management usually plays the major role in identifying a candidate for a position. Says Dow Chemical's Cohen, "If we have a vacancy and we need someone from the US, our president will usually contact the relevant functional head and say that we need a good person for this particular position." Once a candidate is proposed, "the human resources function is responsible for checking the background and suitability of the candidate in question for that position." Although the line manager generally makes the decision about the candidate's job-related qualifications, the human resources manager evaluates the person's longer-term adaptability and ensures that a medical clearance is given. "The immediate supervisor may not have the history that we have in our files," Cohen observes. Thus, the human resources department serves as a cross-check on line management decisions. If the two sides disagree, the appointment will be examined further. But, says Cohen, "within the 15 years in which I've been here at Dow Pacific, I've recommended to veto one move and seriously questioned only four others out of hundreds."

3

Preparation for Overseas Assignments

Executive Summary

To increase the likelihood that executives sent overseas experience successful tours of duty, MNCs are developing comprehensive pre-departure training packages designed to equip employees and their families with the knowledge and skills necessary to function effectively in a foreign environment. These packages, which are often administered by outside vendors, emphasize cross-cultural and language training, as well as instruction in general management and specific operating functions. Many firms also offer executives look-see trips to the destination country and, upon arrival in country, additional training and support.

Although companies agree that successful expatriate assignments are the result of thorough planning and preparation, they differ on how much advance training is really necessary. At one extreme, some MNCs—usually large, long-established global ones, such as *IBM* and *Philips*—offer little or no formal cross-cultural training or leave it to the subsidiary in the destination country. At the other extreme, corporations that are relatively new to the international arena, such as Japan's *NEC*, believe all their expatriates require rigorous predeparture training. NEC puts all departing executives through an extensive integrated training program that comprises area studies, management training and other courses that may last up to six months. Most companies fall in the middle, however, typically offering two, three or five days of preparation.

Predeparture training generally consists of three segments: (1) language instruction, (2) cross-cultural education and (3) look-see trips to the destination country.

Virtually all MNCs provide language instruction, and many actually require it. Look-see visits by the executive and spouse are widely used by companies that send people abroad. These trips provide an initial orientation and a helpful introduction to the routines of daily life in the destination country.

When it comes to cross-cultural training, however, corporate policies differ. Some firms provide cross-cultural training to virtually all expatriates; others offer it only in certain cases. Moreover, the type and extent of training vary considerably, reflecting, in large measure, the extent to which a company has globalized its operations.

In addition to the three basic segments of predeparture training, many companies provide post-arrival training and support to executives and their families. Some use these in-country services as substitutes for predeparture preparation. In other cases, ongoing support services can be quite elaborate and continue throughout an expatriate's entire tour abroad. In-country support may be organized locally or administered long distance with the help of corporate headquarters.

A related issue that concerns MNCs is the extent and nature of predeparture training for LNs brought to work at headquarters. As companies have increased the percentage of LNs employed in their foreign operations and begun to move LNs outside their native countries to development assignments either at world or regional headquarters, devising useful predeparture training packages for LNs has become increasingly important.

Language Training

Whatever else they do, virtually all MNCs give executives as much language training as they can absorb. *IBM*, for example, ensures "that people going to a foreign country, whatever that may mean—a French person moving to the US, a German to Hong Kong, a US citizen to Japan—get whatever language training they need to become proficient," says director of executive resources and development Don Laidlaw. "We also make language instruction available to their spouses." Interestingly, "language training is largely to make the personal lives, rather than the business lives, of overseas employees easier, since English is the common language of our company throughout the world," he says.

- *Colgate-Palmolive*'s director of management and organizational development R. Alicia Whitaker says the importance of having language skills varies by country. In France, she says, "it's fatal not to speak French," adding that the company gave its new vice president for exports at its French subsidiary a six-week, total-immersion course before he ever set foot in France. However, Whitaker says that the need for language fluency in other countries is usually less pressing.

- *General Motors* (GM) is also committed to language training. "We encourage our employees to take about four weeks of full-time immersion training before they leave," says Jim Fisher, staff assistant, international human resources. "And 75–80% of those who take these courses follow up with more study once they're settled in the host country." Language training may be conducted near the executive's current home or elsewhere. "There are pros and cons either way," says Monique Guerrier, GM's director of international human resources. "Some people prefer to get away from the home, the job and all the tasks of getting ready to move while they go through language training. Others find it more convenient to stay near home."

Given the stresses inherent in a move overseas, the company understands that some employees cannot take the time to learn a language beforehand. "We prefer to organize something here before the departure," says Guerrier, "but sometimes, because of the timing, we can't." To deal with the problem, the company uses the services of several external language training firms that offer flexible schedules. "You have people who study the language daily from Monday to Saturday, and you have people who are happier learning the language in one session a week," she explains.

At GM, there is instruction for spouses, as well as expatriates. All language training is one on one and tailored to each person's specific needs. "The spouse needs a vocabulary for daily life—shopping, banking, etc., while the manager needs a business vocabulary," says

Guerrier, "one specific to his or her responsibilities." Fisher emphasizes that instruction is not mandatory, but is highly encouraged.
Ninety-five percent of the company's expatriates take advantage of
these language programs.

- *Dow Chemical*'s Japanese subsidiary offers optional language training for arriving executives and typically allows them to decide
what level of expertise they desire. However, Peter J. Cohen, Dow
Chemical Japan's director of human resources and administrative
services, relates that "my experience in Asia is that European companies are very serious about local language capability." He attributes the difference to the fact that European companies tend to
"send people for much longer periods of time" than their US counterparts, "with little discussion of their repatriation." Indeed, some
European firms even require a rising standard of language proficiency, whereby executives must attain increasingly high standards
of fluency over the course of their assignment. This practice is consistent with the realization of many European companies as a
whole, particularly those based in countries with small domestic
markets, that success abroad is vital to their overall corporate performance.

Some companies offer language training for all employees, even
those not yet slated to go overseas. For example, *Mitsui & Co*, the
giant Japanese general trading company, provides all new employees
with 75–100 hours of English lessons. For the last two decades, the
firm has tested employees on their facility in English, and officials
estimate that 85% of its staff with 11 years of experience or more have
attained the equivalent of a 530 score on the Test of English as a
Foreign Language (TOEFL) exam, just below the 550 required to enter
most US colleges. In addition to English, Mitsui provides Chinese language classes on an ongoing basis and predeparture language training
to prospective overseas assignees.[1]

Cross-Cultural Training

Cross-cultural training is perhaps the main growth area in the training
field, and more and more companies include it as a part of predeparture programs. The primary beneficiaries of this new emphasis on

---

[1]The Japan Overseas Enterprise Association, *The Report of the Research Committee on
International Executive Education* [*Kokusaika yoin ikusei kenkyuiinkai hokokusho*]: Tokyo, May
1990, pp. 120–21.

cross-cultural training are departing executives themselves. But companies stress that spouses and children may benefit as much or even more than executives from this type of instruction, since it is they who are "out" in the local community daily and need to be sensitive to and knowledgeable about the culture. In contrast, most of an executive's time is spent in the somewhat insulated office environment. Therefore, more and more companies have begun offering the training to families as well as executives.

Cross-cultural programs usually take the form of a three-to-five-day immersion course in the assigned country's values, customs and traditions. Although a few companies, such as *Philips*, teach these courses themselves, more often than not (and especially in the US) firms use outside consultants for such instruction. Most consultants have a basic training module for each country, which they tailor to a client company's particular requirements. Moran, Stahl & Boyer (MS&B), for example, begins with a basic program, which becomes more specific depending on client needs. Its three-day predeparture program covers everyday life in the country in question, area studies, doing business in the country, the role of women in the foreign culture, as well as culture shock and the stress executives and their families are likely to experience. Sessions make use of nationals of the country and are designed to prepare executives and their families for situations they will actually encounter (see charts on pp. 54–57). In turn, companies often use more than one consultant, both to ensure they do not become dependent on one supplier and for geographic reasons, since consultants tend to be localized in one country or even region. (Some can, however, run sessions anywhere in the world.) Various consultants specialize in specific cross-cultural topics, e.g., US-Japanese intercultural relations, while others provide a full range of services. (See Appendix for a list of US firms that provide cross-cultural training, and see p. 54 for a cross-cultural training schedule.)

Assessing the Need for Cross-Cultural Training

The amount of predeparture training companies offer is often a question of corporate philosophy and organization, but certain general principles apply.

Degree of Internationalization. A key determinant of predeparture training needs is how routine or, conversely, how unusual, working abroad is at a particular company. Some companies are new to the

Two-Day Cross-Cultural and Area Studies Training Program (Sample Schedule)

Day One

9:00 a.m.   **Welcome and Overview of Cross-Cultural Training**
Orientation to Program Goals and Schedule
Participation and Staff Introductions

9:30   **Profile of Successful Intercultural Adjustment**
This session provides a tangible model and set of targets for successful intercultural adjustment toward which the participants can aspire during their sojourn in the country of assignment.

9:45   **Audiovisual Presentation**
10:15   **Break**

10:30   **Everyday Life in the Country of Assignment**
Presentation and questions and answers regarding the practical details of expatriate life in the country of assignment

12:30 p.m.   **Lunch**

1:45   **Area Studies**
Presentation and questions and answers regarding the practical details of expatriate life in the country of assignment

2:45   **Break**
3:00   **Area Studies**
Presentation on the current events and issues of the country of assignment

4:30   **Debriefing Session**
5:00   **End of Day One**
Homework: Cross-Cultural Analysis Exercise

SOURCE: Moran, Stahl & Boyer, a subsidiary of The Prudential

Day Two

9:00 a.m. **Cross-Cultural Analysis Exercise**

Discussion and analysis of the key cultural differences in values, assumptions and expectations
between both cultures. Representative nationals from
the country of assignment participate in the exercise.

10:30 **Break**

10:45 **Nonverbal Communication Exercise**

Demonstration and discussion of cross-cultural
"body language" in the country of assignment

12:00 **Lunch**

1:15 p.m. **Separate Sessions**

Doing Business in the Country of Assignment. In this
session, local nationals and recently returned expatriate business people identify and discuss with the participants key issues regarding individual and organizational styles of doing business in the country of
assignment.

The Role of Women in the Destination Culture. The
experience of being an expatriate woman in the country of assignment is explored with a recently returned
woman expatriate in terms of social conventions,
education, employment, legal regulations, entertain-
ing and clothing.

Note: *These two sessions are combined if expatriate employee is a
woman.*

3:15 **Cross-Cultural Stress and Shock**

Presentation on the causes, symptoms and strategies
for the management of culture shock, with particular
emphasis on the difficult role of the spouse overseas.
Participants learn to enhance family communication
and support during the transition period.

Note: *This session is modified to include issues relevant to single
expatriates if the participant is not married.*

4:00 **Debriefing and Participant Evaluation of the
Program**

(Continued)

4:30   End of Program

Note: Please keep in mind that it is our practice to tailor our programs to the specific circumstances, needs and requirements of each individual client. Therefore, the designs of our general models are always modified in consultation with the client prior to the delivery of the program.

SOURCE: Moran, Stahl & Boyer, a subsidiary of The Prudential

Training Program Goals

At the conclusion of the program, participants will be able to do the following:

1.   Anticipate the day-to-day activities of life in the new culture and adjust to the differences from their routines at home.

2.   Identify the components of intercultural adjustment and performance and understand these as targets for achievement in the country of assignment.

3.   Describe important historical events that have shaped the national character of the country of assignment.

4.   Identify and discuss current trends and issues in the new country.

5.   Discuss important facts about the country with respect to geography, religion, government and legal systems.

6.   Use the cultural concept, or paradigm, to solve problems and identify how cultural differences can affect social relations with the local nationals of the new country. Anticipate points of conflict and develop problem-solving strategies appropriate to the culture.

7.   Identify, discuss and contrast the differences in cultural values between the two cultures. Use cultural analysis as a technique to deal with cultural differences in business and social relations.

8.   Make successful life style adjustments by engaging in activities that can be transferred to the new culture from their lives at home, as well as new activities unique to living as expatriates.

9. Identify the causes, symptoms and time cycle of culture shock, and engage in activities to successfully manage the process.

10. Recognize the valuable contribution they can make to support the cross-cultural adjustment needs of each other, and use a technique to bring this about during their assignment in the new culture.

11. Explain the concept of nonverbal communication, and describe major ways in which people of the other culture communicate nonverbally.

12. Feel confident and positive about the forthcoming expatriate experience, and enter into it with a positive mind-set and emotional strength.

13. Use strategies to develop appropriate and meaningful social and personal networks that will help their adjustment to the new environment.

SOURCE: Moran, Stahl & Boyer, a subsidiary of The Prudential

international arena or treat international operations essentially as a sideline to their domestic business. Such firms often have delayed going abroad because of a strong domestic market that permitted them to prosper for many years. CEOs and other senior executives of such firms typically have risen to the top within the domestic operation alone, so overseas service is not always a prestigious calling. Typically, executives who hire on with such firms may have had little advance interest in going abroad. When such companies do send executives abroad, they must do more to prepare them than firms that have been active internationally for many years.

For companies with a long history of foreign activities, the situation is often quite different. When a significant percentage of revenues is derived overseas, when a firm's best growth opportunities are outside its home market or when there are large company operations in other countries, international sensitivity is taken for granted and formal predeparture training at headquarters may be viewed as superfluous. An international mind-set is an integral part of the corporate culture, and executives at such firms are *expected* to work abroad at some point in their careers—perhaps several times. Moreover, they usually do a great deal to prepare themselves for overseas service.

Distance and Difference. In general, the newer, smaller and farther away a foreign operation, the more training is advisable before an executive leaves the parent company. Managers sent into the "wilderness" alone—to start a new operation in a fairly remote location, for example—require all the training they can get. Finding a house, getting a driver's license, opening a bank account and so on can all be major challenges without the help of an existing company infrastructure in the country.

When a company does have extensive operations abroad, individual subsidiaries often have sufficient training capabilities of their own to provide much of the instruction and counsel newly arrived managers need. Moreover, a large subsidiary typically has many useful relationships with other local businesses, government bureaucracies, the media and clubs. All of these can help recent arrivals do their jobs better and fit into the community.

However, there is still another consideration that should play an important role in determining the amount and the kind of training an executive receives—the degree of cultural contrast between the corporation's home country (or the home country of the transferring executive) and the destination country. The greater the difference, the more training can help.

Resource People. A key element of most cross-cultural training is exposure of prospective expatriates to "resource people." Typically, these are nationals of the destination country or former expatriates who have worked in that country.

According to Nancy Burgas, manager of global learning systems at *AT&T* with responsibility for predeparture training, "For us, resource people are usually citizens of the country where our executive is going but who have been in the US for several years. They are fluent in English and are familiar with American culture."

In most cases, resource people are provided by the cross-cultural training consultants the company uses, but "if we know of someone who is here from that country or city, we try to get that person involved, too." Given time constraints, however, this can be difficult to arrange. As a result, the company usually relies on the vendor to find good resource people.

Cross-Cultural 'Minimalists'

At *Philips*, in the Netherlands—a country with a population of only 15 million—doing business internationally has been a way of life for decades. Some 93% of the company's revenues come from abroad. Not surprisingly, spending one's whole career in the Netherlands would greatly limit an executive's potential for success. Therefore, most Philips managers look forward to international careers and are comfortable outside their home country before they ever land their first overseas assignment. They have traveled throughout Europe, if not farther afield, and most speak at least one language besides Dutch— usually German or English. Because of this background, the company believes one to two days of formal predeparture training—apart from language training in the required local language—is sufficient.

Similarly, Sweden's *Atlas Copco*, with a home market of about eight million people—about half the size of Philips'—has had even more reason to look abroad. The company's managers consider working overseas glamorous and, more important, highly desirable, because foreign markets are areas of strong growth. Atlas Copco's Swedish managers and even its new recruits are likely to speak English and to have lived, studied or traveled throughout Europe. The company expects its managers to be interested in overseas work and show an aptitude for it. For these reasons, it provides predeparture training only when it sends executives to "exotic" locations, such as the Middle East or Latin America.

Despite a vast domestic market, huge competition caused *Colgate-Palmolive* to turn its attention abroad long ago. "Our particular competence lies in our ability to move products globally," says Colgate's Whitaker. "Over 60% of our revenues come from overseas, where the more profitable segments of our businesses are located." Although the company provides extensive international-oriented training to its younger managers (see Chapter 5), it has little use for predeparture or "garden variety" cross-cultural training for executives. After experimenting with various training modules, "we decided they weren't very useful," says Whitaker. "We have such a large network of subsidiaries—and they have, or know where to find, training resources— that we're better off leaving the instruction to them." For example, the company's general manager in Thailand has found Bangkok firms that are able to provide intercultural orientation programs.

For many of the same reasons as Colgate, *IBM* does not, generally, rely on formal cross-cultural training prior to an executive's departure. The computer giant also has an extensive international network that dates back to a plant established in Canada in the 1930s. "We have IBM people in more than 130 countries," says Laidlaw. "So we really aren't sending people by themselves to cultures that we haven't been able to penetrate." As a result, IBM believes that any country orientation a person needs can be best handled by the host subsidiary. "The general manager in that country may determine that someone new ought to have some personalized training," says Laidlaw. "In such a case, the manager has the responsibility to help that person get what he or she needs."

Cross-Cultural Advocates:
Four Case Studies

In contrast to the firms just mentioned, the companies discussed below are strong believers in predeparture training. In the case of US firms like GM and AT&T, this philosophy may reflect the company's strong domestic presence that has traditionally led executives to look to a domestic career with the company. In the case of Japanese firms, which generally are strong believers in training of all types, in part because of the implicit contract in the lifetime employment system, an emphasis on predeparture training also reflects a strong domestic market. However, the stress on training may also reflect perceptions on the part of top Japanese executives of wide cultural gaps between home and overseas markets, as well as the relative inexperience of many Japan-based MNCs in investing overseas.

Still, not all Japanese firms offer extensive training—and not all Japanese expatriates take advantage of all the training that may be available. The personnel director at the US subsidiary of one Japanese company, upon informally polling Japanese executives assigned to positions in the US, found that some 30% had not received any predeparture training at all. Not a few Japanese executives lamented: "On Monday, my boss said you are going to America. On Tuesday, I got on the plane."

General Motors. At GM, cross-cultural training is one part of a five-step predeparture process designed to cut expatriate failures to virtually nil (see box p. 61). The cross-cultural program, provided by outside vendors, has two segments: (1) factual instruction about the destination; and (2) qualitative issues, such as business etiquette and social customs (even table manners), as well as coping with culture shock, which "everyone experiences at one level or another," says director of international human resources Guerrier.

This part of the course is aimed mainly at "preparing the whole family, including the children, for the transition to the new environment," she says. In these sessions, the family is told in detail what to expect in its new home. "We give them opportunities to react, to

GM: Five Steps to a Successful Foreign Assignment

GM employs a five-step program that helps executives and their families make an informed decision about whether to accept an overseas position and, later, helps them cope successfully with the adjustments they must make in such assignments. The process is:

- *Selection.* Using a proprietary data base, GM identifies candidates, and then, working with the specific functional area that does the hiring, selects the person to whom the job will be offered.

- *Orientation day.* "The employee and spouse spend a full day with us here in our department," says GM's Guerrier. "We organize a series of meetings with staff experts in many areas to give them information necessary to help them make their decision. Some of the questions we answer for them are: How will they be treated as expatriate families? What kind of compensation, premiums and benefits are they going to receive? What kind of relocation assistance can we give them?" She emphasizes that this is a purely informational exercise, and candidates are under no obligation to make their preferences known about the assignment under discussion. Also during the orientation day, an informal assessment is made regarding the adaptability skills of the employee and spouse. This is done through personal discussions with the couple.

- *A look-see visit.* Lasting about three to five business days, "the look-see trip has two purposes," says Guerrier. "The first is to give the employee the opportunity to meet his or her boss, colleagues and staff, to assess job conditions and work expectations and to learn more about the local business environment. The second purpose is for the couple to look at the host city and country from the perspective of their family and to begin to get a feel for living conditions and essential services, like hospitals and schools." When candidates return from a look-see visit, they must formally decide to accept or decline the assignment.

- *Cross-cultural training.* As described above, this is, in GM's view, the most important of the five steps. It focuses on a combination of facts and advice from experienced trainers and resource people.

(Continued)

> - *Immersion language training.* Language is a key part of the program, but, as described above, while the company prefers that executives undergo immersion training, it also permits them to space out language training. In addition, executives are encouraged to continue training after arrival in the foreign country.
>
> More than 90% of the candidates who go through orientation day accept an international post, says Guerrier. The payoff is also measurable: The expatriate failure rate is less than 1%.

adjust, to understand what moving to a new country entails," says Guerrier. To communicate the real picture, former expatriates are used as resource people.

As with language training, cross-cultural training may be offered in the executive's place of employment, or the executive and family may be flown to a centralized cross-cultural training location. Wherever it takes place, GM's cross-cultural training is "not a canned program for a whole group of people" but is specifically tailored for each family. The company believes such training is one key to the success or failure of a family's adjustment to a foreign posting. "We consider it more important than language training," says Guerrier. "If we have to prioritize, we prefer to have the cross-cultural training program with our people before their departure. For us, it's more important that we give them the skills to adjust to the shock of a new culture. We know that when they arrive in a foreign country, the family members can devote their attention to language training."

AT&T. AT&T is one of many companies that prospered domestically in the past, but now looks abroad for its future growth. The US telecommunications leader is vigorously expanding into foreign markets and has made a major commitment to predeparture expatriate training. Most senior AT&T executives have spent their entire careers in the US, so those who serve abroad are blazing a trail for the company. AT&T intends to provide these executives with all the services they need. "Since we're new to this, we've tried to do it right," says manager of global learning systems Burgas.

The firm uses the program developed by consultants MS&B to provide training for departing expatriates and their families. The program, which normally lasts three days, can be extended to five. It provides detailed information on the assigned country's business and social environment and on relocation services. The family also meets with one or more resource people. In most cases, the program is conducted at MS&B's international headquarters in Boulder, Colorado, four weeks before departure. AT&T has found that sending the entire family to Boulder relaxes the family and removes them from a stressful situation, i.e., selling or renting their home, packing, saying goodbye to relatives and friends and otherwise getting ready to go abroad. "It's time set aside for them just to deal with their move," says Burgas.

The AT&T program covers a number of areas in three well-defined segments. "The first is about business, including the nature of office work in the destination country, hierarchical relationships and general business practices and etiquette," says Burgas. For example, a manager would need to know whether meetings are held on time and whether people volunteer their opinions or have to be asked. "Another part deals with the details of everyday living," she says. "Since the spouse is usually the wife, a women's resource person, typically the wife of a US expatriate currently in that country, would come in and share her knowledge and impressions about shopping, health care, education and local transportation." In addition, "There is a third part that deals with the psychological adjustment necessary to cope with 'culture shock'," adds Burgas.

At one recent session Burgas attended for a family going to Tokyo, "the resource person was accompanied by some of our Japanese employees working here in the US, and they were able to tell more about the Japanese culture—gift-giving traditions, what you do when you first move into your neighborhood, how to celebrate holidays and what is customary for an American to do in a variety of practical situations," says Burgas.

NEC. The Tokyo-based Nippon Electric Corp (NEC) is one of Japan's leading companies in expatriate training. The computer and electronics manufacturer has developed a comprehensive predeparture training program for its executives and any other NEC employee going on overseas assignment that begins six months before they leave Japan. Unlike the predeparture packages that are most popular with US-based companies, NEC integrates specific predeparture material with a formidable array of other internationally flavored management training courses, many of which are open to all employees (see box p. 64).

After carrying out various educational and training programs for many years, the firm established the NEC Institute of Management in 1983 to coordinate future corporate training activities. Based in Tokyo, the institute does utilize some "external specialists"—rang-

NEC: Promoting Globalization at Home

As part of a general corporate effort to promote globalization, NEC has devised an ongoing cross-cultural training process. The company brings a small number of local nationals in overseas NEC subsidiaries to its Tokyo headquarters for two- to four-year study and work programs. After a period of study at the NEC Institute for Management, the foreign nationals work in various departments (usually in the marketing or engineering fields) to improve their understanding of NEC and to upgrade their particular skills. Although the company will pay for foreigners to learn Japanese, they are encouraged to speak English in the office. The point of this is to "internationalize" the work environment by exposing Japanese staff to people from other cultures.

Management's theory is that the presence of foreign nationals at headquarters will expose Japanese employees to new ideas and assist in language training, principally for the Japanese staff. "Not everyone at NEC can have the experience of an overseas assignment, so having people who speak English among our colleagues gives them a minimum level of equivalent exposure to a foreign culture," says NEC's Yamamoto.

ing from native English-language speakers to professors in management from nearby universities—to help conduct some of the actual training sessions, along with NEC staffers on a full-time or part-time basis.

The core of the predeparture program is language training. "Based on training in linguistic skills, we can go on to cross-cultural and other aspects of international communication skills training," explains Masaru Yamamoto, general manager of the international education division of the NEC Institute of Management. After completing basic international communications training, prospective overseas assignees take courses to improve their international management skills. Besides courses for senior- and middle-level managers, programs include classes on basic and advanced trade practices, overseas project planning, international finance, insurance, legal affairs, accounting and marketing. "In our area study category, we also offer courses on business practices in North America, Asia and Europe, as well as the Middle East, Oceania, Latin America and Africa," adds Yamamoto. Among the more interesting courses are a class discussing equal employment opportunity laws and practices in the US and a special predeparture session for spouses. While on overseas assignment, managers and staffers can also participate in correspondence courses (see NEC's Alternatives to Overseas Training Centers, in Chapter 4) and look forward to a reentry program upon their return (see Chapter 6, Strategies for Successful Repatriation).

"We give an orientation to each manager selected for an overseas assignment," explains Yamamoto, "in which our staff goes over the courses one by one." The company has also prepared a handbook covering the offerings.

NEC's international education program is organized into mandatory and optional courses. Because the range of available options is vast, each employee's program is individually tailored to his needs. Ultimately, "the manager himself makes the decision on what to include in his program, in consultation with his direct and immediate supervisor." The time spent on such educational activities "depends on the combination chosen," Yamamoto says. "Also, some of the managers going abroad are very experienced; area study courses, for example, may not always be necessary."

Management doubts that this system could be easily exported to non-Japanese companies, or even to its own subsidiaries outside Japan, because it operates in the context of the Japanese lifetime employment system. "Our foreign subsidiaries' employment systems are based, in many cases, on the assumption that people job hop," says Hajime Hasegawa, senior vice president and director of the NEC Institute of Management. Even though extensive international education programs clearly have numerous benefits, they are more difficult to justify financially outside the context of the lifetime employment system.

Dow Chemical Japan. Dow Chemical Japan offers cross-cultural training to arriving expatriates. Expatriates from the US to Tokyo first receive about a week's worth of orientation at home before departure. Upon arrival, they may go through a two- to three-day program on cross-cultural management issues. Courses are offered when enough people would stand to benefit from them to justify their expense. Dow Chemical's Cohen emphasizes that his program is geared toward a relatively small number of expatriates in circumstances that would make a more ambitious program less than cost effective. Moreover, in contrast with some firms, Dow prefers to offer cross-cultural training after expatriate executives have had time to get their feet wet. "I prefer that the program be run about three months after the person arrives here, so that he's got some experience under his belt and will know what the lecturers or trainers are talking about when they bring up potential problems," Cohen explains. Afterwards, Cohen encourages executives to attend symposiums, lectures and programs on topics related to business management and practices in Japan. Although Cohen publicizes such events among managers, the company does not organize such activities itself. Like many other firms, Dow Chemical Japan hires an orientation company, Tokyo General Agency, to assist new arrivals with the exigencies of daily life during the first six weeks of their tour.

Look-See Visits

An important part of the predeparture process at many MNCs, usually administered after an executive has already been offered a foreign post, is the look-see trip. On such trips, executives, sometimes with their families, travel to their potential destinations to examine conditions firsthand. Candidates are normally instructed that the trip is an opportunity to learn about the country from the point of view of someone who will live there, not a tourist holiday. Many firms provide a local "helper"—either someone from the subsidiary's personnel department or the spouse of an expatriate already living there—to show the candidate around and provide relevant information.

- *GM* gives all departing expatriates and their spouses a look-see visit as part of its five-step program. Philips sends executives to their destination cities for a few days, depending on how useful it thinks such a visit may be.

- *IBM*, in contrast, only allows look-see visits for remote or unusual locations, but what constitutes "remote" is relative. "There are certain parts of the world where we think this is necessary," says IBM's Laidlaw. "An American going to Tokyo or Singapore might need to go there for a short tour, but a trip isn't usually required for Europe, since most people have been there." Conversely, "an Australian being sent to Tokyo or Singapore might not need a look see" there, but might benefit from one if under consideration for a post in South America.

In-Country Assistance

As discussed earlier, post-arrival language training is fairly common at most companies as is post-arrival cross-cultural training, which is discussed in Chapter 4. The following, however, can also prove valuable to expatriates, either in lieu of or as a complement to predeparture training.

- *Local organizations.* In addition to the range of training and support services the company's own overseas subsidiaries can offer to new arrivals, many MNCs also tap the network of programs provided by local organizations. For example, the American Institute in Taiwan (which acts as the unofficial US representation on Taiwan, since the latter does not have diplomatic relations with Washington) sponsors cross-cultural training sessions that are attended by executives and managers from many US corporations. Another local resource is the Community Service Center (CSC), organized by members of the US expatriate community in Taipei. David Wang, *NCR Taiwan*'s manager of personnel relations, relates that CSC "produced a videotape to help overseas assignees employed in Taiwan become familiar with the local environment quickly." CSC provides each incoming foreigner—regardless of nationality—with a copy of the tape. NCR Taiwan also reimburses all tuition fees for the family members of expatriate employees who wish to learn Chinese.

  Company membership in or sponsorship of such groups can help improve the social amenities for expatriates. At NCR Taiwan, "if employees join the Taipei American Club, the company reimburses the fees because we hope they can make friends here," says Wang. "By helping keep people happy, such benefits also make them more productive on the job."

- *Company get-togethers.* Some MNCs also have found it beneficial to hold conferences, meetings or other forums that bring expatriates and their families together. Often expatriates and TCNs who meet at such gatherings go on to network and socialize on their own. For example, a few years ago, *AT&T* sponsored a forum for wives of expatriates in its international communications business unit, the firm's largest overseas business operation, in Europe.

  "The managing directors were going to have a meeting in Switzerland, and we decided to invite the spouses as well," says AT&T's Nancy Burgas. "With help from our cross-cultural consultants, Moran, Stahl & Boyer, we put on a two-day program for them that dealt primarily with cultural issues, adaptation to their host countries and stress reduction."

- *Publications.* Publications are another way to keep expatriates and their families in touch with headquarters as well as one another. Indeed, when the above-mentioned meeting at *AT&T* came to an end, it had been so successful, says AT&T's Burgas, "that afterward, the women got together and started *Worldwise,* a quarterly newsletter to keep in touch with each other," which is still being published today. The newsletter features travel tips, things to do when visiting various cities in Europe and advertisements to help expatriate families swap houses during vacations. There is even a teen column to help young people in the same country or elsewhere in Europe become pen pals.

  The newsletter lists on the back page all the AT&T business unit spouses in each country. "Now, when any new spouse comes into a country," says Burgas, "you can be assured that other women are going to know about her and take her under their wing."

  Dow Chemical also uses publications to keep its far-flung executives in touch. Though it has not developed a special publication for executives abroad, it has arranged for expatriates to receive local divisional and employee news from their units back home, in addition to the usual corporate materials. Thus, "people from Europe get European news, and people from Australia get Australian news," explains Dow Chemical Japan's Cohen.

- *Parent company services.* In some instances, the parent company continues to offer assistance to its international employees and their families. *NEC's* overseas personnel division in Tokyo provides expatriates with "health insurance, publications and a supply of Japanese food when they go to countries where it's difficult to obtain such foods," says NEC's Hasegawa. Another area in which headquarters plays an active role is the education of expatriates' children. Because Japanese children educated abroad often have difficulty gaining entrance to the best schools in Japan, given that country's system of high-school and college examinations, NEC has retained an "education consultant." Parents can call the consultant from abroad to discuss their children's schooling; the consultant also travels periodically to NEC subsidiaries and branches overseas to work directly with families.

- *Medical services.* Medical assistance is one area in which company support can literally spell the difference between life and death. Apart from differences in health standards, language and cultural problems can make it difficult to obtain high-quality health care abroad. With this in mind, companies may wish to actually assign doctors to particularly remote locations. In addition, larger installations, even in large foreign cities, may justify keeping one or more doctors on staff. At the very least, a company should be aware of local doctors who speak the corporate language and are accredited at local hospitals in order to provide employees with referrals. Many companies subscribe to the SOS Medical Alert Service, a private company that provides emergency medical transport worldwide.

NEC, for example, has "more than 10 staff doctors," says Hasegawa. "One of their functions is to travel to our foreign subsidiaries to carry out health checks. This lets our staff abroad feel at ease, because they can consult with them in Japanese and not face difficulties in discussing health problems in a foreign language." In addition, "if our company doctor finds any major problems with a staff member on overseas assignment, he is authorized to ask headquarters to bring the person home for treatment."

Even if a company does not sponsor doctors, providing money for medical care, on a liberal basis, can reduce employee stress. Treatment of stress itself is another area in which companies should be willing to foot the bill. For example, *Dow Chemical Japan*'s Cohen says, "if a problem is medically related, our insurance will usually cover the fees." In addition, the company has established relations with counselors whom it can recommend to executives suffering from unusual psychological stress.

Predeparture Training for Local Nationals

Although most companies are sensitive to the need for predeparture training for expatriates and TCNs, the same cannot always be said for LNs who transfer to headquarters. (Obviously, when LNs are assigned to countries other than their own or the company's home base, they become TCNs, and at most firms, get the full range of training offered to TCNs.) Companies vary in the degree they differentiate between employees from the home country and those from abroad. When companies do not distinguish between the two, as at *IBM*, it bodes well for treatment of LNs who are expatriated to headquarters. When a company maintains a strong center of gravity at home, however, all too often LNs receive short shrift.

Dow Chemical Japan: Training Local Nationals

Until about 1986, Dow Chemical Japan had no special training program for departing local nationals. As more Japanese nationals began
to go overseas, however, the firm has developed a program that is
centered on language training, but also incorporates cross-cultural
training, including seminars for the executive's spouse. Particular
emphasis is placed on teaching presentation skills, an area in which—
at least by US standards—Japanese executives are rather weak.
"Giving presentations is not a skill that Japanese employees have traditionally had to use," observes Dow Chemical's Cohen. His human
resources and administrative services department thus offers classes
with the assistance of consultants—featuring audiovisual aids and
role-playing—to departing Japanese staffers on presentation methods
commonly used in the US. Besides language, the style and length of
such events may pose problems. In particular, Japanese executives
may be unaccustomed to taking critical questions from an audience.

In addition, Dow Chemical Japan provides departing local nationals with all the English language training it can. To measure employee progress, the firm uses the FSI or Foreign Service Institute tests.
Such tests provide a standardized rating of an executive's ability that
can be useful when sending an executive to locations unaccustomed
to nonnative speakers. Notes Cohen, people often do not grasp how
difficult learning a foreign language can be. Therefore, besides ensuring that a foreign executive's language proficiency is up to an acceptable standard, "once these tests are passed, they also tell a receiving
supervisor that this person's English is at an acceptable level. If
there's a problem, it might be with the supervisor himself. He may
need to exercise more patience."

In addition to predeparture training, Dow Chemical also provides
executives arriving to foreign posts with an orientation consultant
who helps them with such things as housing and education.
Facilitating social integration in the new locale often becomes the
responsibility of the executives' supervisor. However, at least at
Dow's headquarters in Midland, Michigan, there is a fairly large
corps of international employees.

Although Cohen believes the firm does a good job of preparing and educating local nationals bound for the US, programs for other destinations are less developed. "If we send someone to Europe, I'm not sure we have a sufficient program to cover how to work in Germany or other countries," he acknowledges. Upon the return of Japanese nationals from assignments, however, Dow Chemical Japan asks each returning local expatriate to complete an evaluation sheet that covers how well they were prepared and how they were received. In turn, that information is cycled back to the supervisor in the US, as well as to Dow's international transfers function at Midland. The company has found this procedure very useful in its efforts to improve its local national transfers process.

Few subsidiaries offer the same predeparture training to employees en route to other countries as does the home office for its outward-bound staff. Home offices often neglect employees who come in from foreign locations for three major reasons:

- Historically, most companies are more accustomed to sending expatriates out from headquarters than they are to bringing in people from the overseas operations.

- Companies sometimes incorrectly assume that it is easier to cope with the headquarters environment than with an "exotic" foreign location—although headquarters can be equally exotic to those from another country.

- Expatriates leaving the home country typically assume high-level positions and can count on subordinates in overseas locations to help them. Foreigners coming to corporate headquarters typically occupy lower-level positions and are on their own. Indeed, one company notes that when foreign employees arrive in the parent company's home city in the US, they have to clear customs and immigration, rent cars and find their way to the hotel, with no assistance from the company.

At IBM, assignees from any country to another are considered identical. Hence, expatriates from Hong Kong to the US are treated the same as those going from the US to Hong Kong. The situation is similar at Coca-Cola, where, says Director of Human Resources Development Kroh, "we have attempted to implement a 'buddy system,' in which employees entering from a foreign affiliate are paired up with employees at headquarters to help make the visitors feel at home." Incoming people also receive English training. In addition, the company contracts with "professional people in the Atlanta area to work with our foreign staff members and help them get their children into the right schools," he says.

Companies could easily do more for incoming LNs. Helpful practices might include such things as predeparture training in their home countries or post-arrival training in the headquarters country, ongoing support services and intensive language training—in short, the same methods that have proven beneficial to expatriates and TCNs departing for new assignments.

4

Continuing International Training

Executive Summary

MNCs are learning that it is not enough to train executives only once—for their initial overseas posts—and then expect them to function effectively for years and develop into seasoned internationalists. Training must continue over an executive's entire career, and the training that managers receive must be tailored to their specific needs and career paths. By honing their cross-cultural, substantive skills and offering them advanced management training, companies can help ensure that their managers are fully prepared for each new international assignment.

The struggle of large corporations to avoid bureaucratic constraints has increased the need for employees who have the flexibility to complete assignments in a variety of geographic settings. The ability of international managers to adapt to changing business circumstances is a necessity now that operational responsibility—the power to make decisions—has been pushed further and further down the managerial ladder.

Companies are discovering that training executives during an international assignment not only ensures that managers retain the technical skills they need to perform their jobs, but also promotes awareness of such key corporate values as independence and responsibility. Like other corporate functions, executive training has taken on an increasingly global dimension in recent years.

MNCs typically identify several areas of training that have particularly strong international components. Besides highly specific predeparture and language training, which were discussed in Chapter 3, international training programs generally fall into three categories:

- *Cross-cultural training* encompassing social interaction with people from other cultures and training in foreign business practices (see Appendix for a list of selected cross-cultural resources available in the US).

- *Substantive skills training* in matters such as finance and marketing.

- *Advanced management training* consisting of sending employees to prestigious, often university-run programs. These are usually reserved for more senior executives, on assorted management topics.

Apart from these three categories, MNCs are devoting more resources to training LNs, as befits their increased importance in the corporate hierarchy. The training of LNs can take all the forms just mentioned, yet presents its own special challenges.

Types of International Training

Cross-Cultural Training

Overtly international, this type of executive training includes soft training in cultural differences—particularly in working with or managing people from other cultures—as well as harder training on social, economic and business conditions in international markets, often with an eye to comparative differences. At many companies, executives attend courses on particular countries, such as the countries where they currently serve, other countries in the region or those of their next assignments.

Although most companies insist that headquarters establish the overall direction of training programs to ensure adequate quality control, when it comes to a standard course on "doing business in" a particular country, the content and approach are generally left to the overseas operating subsidiaries. The rationale is that subsidiaries are best suited to decide what is important to teach and, therefore, should supervise the instruction.

Even when companies set up regional training centers to hold such courses, the instructors or teaching plans usually come from the country being studied rather than from the regional management group. This high level of decentralization reflects the view of most companies and that training is a needs-driven discipline.

US.   US firms usually offer some cross cultural training.

- *AT&T* Europe, like many large US MNCs, possesses a major training center in Europe. Although the firm's Brussels training center serves as an important resource for the entire region, when it comes to managing specific "doing business in" courses, the local country organizations usually take the initiative. "They're most in touch with the local needs," says Bibiana Santiago, AT&T's human resources director for Europe, the Middle East and Africa. Indeed, such courses are normally held in the individual countries where employees are located. The chief requirement, set by headquarters, is that the local subsidiary demonstrate that a sufficient number of managers need to take the course, usually at least six. When that requirement is met, the local subsidiary—sometimes working with the regional headquarters—may either arrange for an outside company to develop a course or develop one internally.

  It is particularly important that courses at the local level provide cross-cultural comparisons and address issues from both the host country's and the foreign company's perspectives. For example, recalls AT&T's manager of global learning systems Nancy Burgas, "We did a 'Marketing in Japan' course one time. It was organized by an outside vendor. We got in a Japanese advertising agency and showed videotapes of the way they advertise in Japan versus what we do in the US. We had Japanese resource people involved in marketing ventures talk about the way they would approach a problem and contrast this with the US approach."

  Like other AT&T training centers, including those in the US, London and Singapore, AT&T's Brussels facility has developed relationships with private training vendors. "We work with vendors in the UK and Belgium and, indeed, countries throughout the region," says Santiago. At the same time, AT&T can also send out instructors from the US or a regional training center to fulfill a specific need on the part of an individual business unit anywhere in the world. The business units, in turn, are capable of tailoring courses to meet their own needs. Typical subjects include doing business in France, marketing in Japan and negotiating skills.

Europe. In contrast to most US companies, European companies are generally more sparing in their use of cross-cultural training.

- *Atlas Copco,* the highly global Swedish company, for example, does not emphasize cross-cultural training—perhaps because its executives are expected to possess considerable intercultural sensitivity from the outset. In response to a specific need, however, the company will organize a course on an ad hoc basis. As at AT&T, such training is usually locally driven. For example, several years ago, the company invested in Ets Georges Renault, a small, locally oriented French firm. Managers from Atlas Copco Tools AB, a company in the same line of business as the acquired one, had to work closely with French management, and to avoid friction, the company decided to provide managers with cross-cultural training. "We provided training to the Swedes on how to deal with the French and to the French on how to deal with the Swedes and others abroad," says Nils-Åke Jenstav, vice president of group staff personnel.

- *Philips* of the Netherlands, similarly, offers comparatively little cross-cultural training. Executives are expected to possess cultural understanding as a matter of course. The cross-cultural training it does offer is incorporated into its general training courses. These courses are cross cultural in two important ways: (1) The material included in courses is usually applicable to more than one country and thus free of ethno- or cultural centrism; and (2) courses are often given to executives from many countries and must use examples and teaching methods that can be easily understood by people from various national, ethnic and cultural backgrounds.

Japan. If European companies on the whole practice less cross-cultural training than their US counterparts, some leading Japanese companies practice more—perhaps because they perceive substantial cultural differences between Japanese society and many of its overseas markets.

- *MEI.* Officials at Matsushita Electric Industrial (MEI), for example, have found that its overseas assignees, particularly those sent to the US, benefit from continuing training in cross-cultural subjects after they arrive overseas. "There are some areas that are difficult to teach here in Japan before overseas assignees leave," says Nobuo Umeoka, assistant general manager for the corporate personnel department at MEI's Osaka headquarters. A case in point concerns law. "For example, in Japan, we normally regard water as a natural gift that we can utilize without any expense, but in many other countries, these resources are regarded in a more legalistic way and are subject to contracts." Japanese expatriates must learn this upon arrival in the US. Matsushita and other Japanese firms also require executives bound for the US to take a course on US equal employment opportunity laws (see box pp. 80-81), and other US labor-related legal requirements and practices.

In addition to training courses for executives on permanent assignment, it may prove beneficial to set up a special training course, from time to time, for an executive group that is being sent abroad on temporary assignment. For example, if a group of US businessmen is going to work on a specific project in Japan, a company might set up a course just for these executives. Given the expense of sending a group overseas for a short period and the fact that a large project may be at stake, such training can be quite cost effective. Similarly, Japanese firms often set up special programs for executive groups that are going overseas.

■ *Fuji Xerox.* Through 1990, over 200 Fuji Xerox employees per year attended intercultural communication courses at its Learning Institute in Tokyo to improve their skills in communicating with non-Japanese colleagues and clients. The trainee process, however, was neither centrally regulated nor systematic. To train and internationalize the work force in a more systematic manner, Fuji Xerox has developed its Internationalization Education Program (see box p. 82).

Budgeting Time for Training

To ensure that executives receive the training they need, some companies have established training "accounts" for every management employee. Each manager is expected to use up this account in the form of days spent on training activities.

■ *Bull,* the large French manufacturer of computers and electronic systems, is a company that uses this approach. To formalize its commitment to provide executives with ample training, Bull mandates that executives prepare a training budget, which includes a minimum of 10 full days of coursework each year.

"Each manager, anywhere in the world, has the opportunity to have his own training plan and the opportunity to select different

Fujitsu America: Fashioning an Orientation Package for Arriving Executives

Until recently, Fujitsu Ltd operated under the assumption that arriving executives received most, if not all, the training they needed before departure. Upon analyzing training actually received, however, Fujitsu America Inc (FAI), headquartered in San Jose, California, decided to beef up post-arrival education and support. Following are some elements of the new program:

- *Language training.* To supplement language training executives may have already received in Japan, FAI provided (on a pilot basis for a three-month period) a supplemental English as a Second Language (ESL) program for Japanese expatriates. Since most Japanese study English in high school, their knowledge of grammar and general reading ability are often quite advanced. Problems occur more frequently in actual conversation or in listening to (as well as giving) presentations. For anyone learning a foreign language, spoken idioms are often the most difficult to understand. FAI's ESL pilot program offered newly arrived Japanese executives two to three months of instruction, with classes held twice a week. Besides hiring English-language instructors from a nearby community college, FAI found US employees willing to volunteer to teach classes on American idioms. Although the program's costs were primarily borne by the company, assignees were asked to pay about $260–280 for the program, in part to ensure attendance.

- *Family orientation.* FAI is also working on a personalized orientation program for families of arriving Japanese assignees. Rather than leave orientation to associates to perform on an informal basis, a bilingual employee associated with FAI's human resources department (a Japanese-born American woman) visits newly arrived families and advises family members, especially the wife, on how to adapt to life in the San Jose area. Among other things, she encourages them to participate in community activities and organizations.

- *Equal employment opportunity law courses.* Like some other US subsidiaries of Japanese firms, FAI now provides expatriates to the US with special training on US equal employment opportunity (EEO) statutes. "The concepts of EEO and affirmative action are still a little foreign in Japan," explains John Klinestiver, FAI's vice president of human resources. Although Japan passed an equal employment opportunity law in 1985, several aspects of the Japanese law, its implementation and cultural context differ from that of the US. "Because it's a hot issue here, we want to make doubly sure that arriving executives from Japan are familiar with US laws and policies so that they do not find themselves in awkward positions," Klinestiver explains.

  FAI's one-day EEO course provides newly arrived executives with an introduction to key EEO-related statutes and presents a few case studies on the application of EEO principles. Included are lectures, a bilingual video presentation by an attorney specializing in EEO practice and a lengthy discussion session. Thus far, the class has been well received by those who have taken it at Fujitsu, including ranking Japanese managers at both the senior vice president and vice president levels.

- *Training manuals.* FAI has just finished compiling a manual on a topic most US executives take for granted—how to manage and utilize secretaries. "It seems kind of odd," notes Klinestiver, "but many Japanese executives have never been overseas before and are not familiar with the role of secretaries in US companies. As a result, many are not sure what they should—or should not—ask secretaries to do." For example, in Japan, executives in some companies still expect "office ladies" to make sure that there's tea on their desks when they arrive at work in the morning. A manager who expected the same from a US secretary would be disappointed, at best. Alternatively, says Klinestiver, "the Japanese manager may be unaware of how much he can delegate to an American secretary." As a result, secretaries may be left just sitting around making travel arrangements and miscellaneous telephone calls, because the manager doesn't realize that he may involve the secretary more deeply in his work on a day-to-day basis. Says Klinestiver, "We believe that this manual—which is written in Japanese—should help Japanese managers utilize their secretaries more effectively."

Fuji Xerox: Institutionalizing the Work Force

To help promote global thinking among its work force and to develop a pool of employees who are capable of working and conducting business overseas by 1999," Fuji Xerox has fashioned a unique, completely voluntary Internationalization Education Program that is offered to employees who may or may not be going overseas any time soon. As such, the program represents a broad investment in the future of the company. It contains the following nine principal facets, which are deliberately *not* listed in any particular order:

- A registry system (a voluntary testing procedure to assess employee international and cross-cultural knowledge);
- An overseas training program;
- Fuji-Xerox language certification tests;
- Language school;
- Correspondence courses;
- Self-initiated study (at Japanese colleges and universities);
- A language consultant program;
- In-house English-language training; and
- Seminars on intercultural communications and awareness.

Combined with an extensive system of training in functional skills, this program aims to produce "internationalized corporate employees" who can "clearly express opinions—in a foreign language as well as Japanese—based on broad knowledge, with a deep understanding and tolerance for other cultures, combined with an ability to accomplish work, achieve coexistence with local people and contribute to the growth of international society as well as Fuji Xerox and the Xerox group," says a company brochure on the educational program.

Although such training might strike some observers as marginal, the company believes it will pay large dividends in years to come. Indeed, while some of the stated goals may seem amorphous, the training should help Fuji Xerox compete internationally. Not the least of its benefits will be the development of a pool of managers and employees who will be available—and fairly well trained for—future overseas assignments.

It also aims to reduce the existing communications gap between Fuji Xerox's Japanese staff and the parent company's US and European employees by providing a wider and more prolonged cross-cultural experience than is available during predeparture training.

NEC: Training by Satellite

NEC's latest effort to bring the benefits of training to its expatriate work force is a pilot satellite educational program. Made possible by proprietary NEC technology, this program not only opens opportunities to facilitate intracompany education programs, but, as a test of the advanced satellite broadcasting technology and conference arrangements, may provide the basis for future business. Although the satellite training program has been used only once—in October 1989—the company plans to utilize it again in the future.

In its single use, "we had an interactive link between Tokyo and Singapore over the Intelsat satellite for a three-day period," says Hajime Hasegawa, senior vice president and director of the NEC Institute of Management. "About 30 managers from our Asian affiliates gathered in Singapore. We began by sending presentations from Tokyo, including a report on technological developments by researchers at headquarters, a speech by NEC President Tadahiro Sekimoto on our company's management philosophies and other discussions of corporate strategy and total quality-control policies." In turn, adds Hasegawa, the senior management of NEC's affiliate in Singapore "served as the instructors for an area study program on Southeast Asia." The exercise cost ¥4 million (about $28,200 at the then-current exchange rate of about ¥142:$1) in line expenses.

Although time zones present certain obstacles to the system's expansion to NEC offices in the Americas, Europe and Africa, "satellite communication will be the fashion for the next era," Hasegawa believes.

courses, both internal or external," says Bull's executive training manager. This means executives have considerable leeway in planning their individual training budgets. For example, Bull is willing to authorize a complete international training course for one executive, if that is the only way the executive can obtain the needed instruction.

Bull expects every manager in the corporate section to develop and complete a tailored training plan every year. The plan is devised jointly by the manager, his superior and the training manager in human resources.

■ *IBM* also insists that its executives follow an annual training schedule. "Every manager is required to take 40 hours of instruction per year, of which 32 hours must focus on the management of people," says Don Laidlaw, director of executive resources and development. IBM's considerable training offerings may be divided into two categories. First, the firm offers training in being a manager, i.e., training in the management of people. Second, the firm provides functional training, i.e., training in communications, finance, personnel, technical (in the sense of scientific) subjects and marketing. Both types of training are offered at IBM's training centers around the world.

Substantive Skills Training

Almost all large companies regularly teach such basic management functions as sales, marketing, finance and production, as well as topics in specialized fields, such as labor relations, taxation and environmental compliance. As companies have expanded abroad, however, the task of upgrading executive knowledge in these areas has assumed an increasingly international cast. Although the overall corporate trend is toward offering more training of all kinds, many companies, as a special priority, are beefing up the international side of their training, i.e., placing subjects in an international context. In addition, substantive training is no longer offered only to executives at headquarters. As more and more companies become multinational, overseas training efforts have come to match those at headquarters, thus providing MNCs with true global training capabilities and reflecting the greater importance of LNs in human resources planning.

■ *Philips,* for example, estimates that half its management training at the corporate level is oriented toward students from more than one culture. To satisfy their diverse needs, courses must be free of any parochial orientation. Such "cosmopolitanism," however, is only one side of the coin. Training in such fields as marketing and finance can also take on an international dimension when it covers specific regions or countries other than the Netherlands. Typically, the subject matter matches location and type of business. For example, executives might attend a course on marketing as it applies to a particular region, at a regional training center, or as it applies to a particular business, at the product division itself. Alternatively, expatriates might take a course in finance in the country where they are currently stationed. Unlike cross-cultural courses, which are given on a more ad hoc basis, courses in marketing and finance are often offered as a regular part of the curriculum.

- *IBM*, like many other major corporations, has invested in several regional management-training centers worldwide. At the same time, however, the company has also created specialized facilities for subjects such as finance and personnel. "We have a campus in Briarcliff Manor, New York, which is managed by finance," says IBM's Laidlaw. "They train our financial people based here in North America in a whole series of courses throughout the year." Meanwhile, financial personnel in Europe are instructed at an IBM facility outside of Brussels. "Courses are international," says Laidlaw, "but international only in the sense that they are offered worldwide. The difference between finance as it's conducted in Europe and here would be addressed" by virtue of differences in curriculum.

  On the one hand, "we recognize that our managers need to think from the point of view of the region or the entire worldwide operation, not only from that of their own unit," says Laidlaw. "So a course taught in Brussels, for example, deals with all the European countries." At the same time, managers also need concrete information on practices in specific countries. "Country-specific issues are always addressed within the country itself," he says.

- *NEC*, the Japanese computer and electronics giant, has centralized much of its training in its NEC Institute of Management in Tokyo. Masaru Yamamoto, the institute's general manager for international education, believes that manufacturing companies in Japan are putting more effort into international training than many firms in the service sector, such as some of Japan's giant general trading companies (*sogo shosha*).

  Companies long involved in international trade or finance tend to attract prospective employees interested in world affairs and often with strong language capabilities. Managers and technicians involved in manufacturing activity traditionally have had fewer opportunities to travel abroad, interact with foreigners or learn foreign languages. The recent acceleration of direct Japanese investment abroad, whether into North American, European or Asian markets, has also entailed a flood of technology transfer or technical assistance agreements. Most of these pacts require Japanese specialists in fields from manufacturing management to product design to spend considerable time abroad. The result is a rapidly expanding demand in manufacturing firms for international education.

Along with other leading Japanese firms, NEC believes that its investment in an elaborate educational programs is worthwhile, because "it is based on the Japanese lifelong employment system," says Hajime Hasegawa, senior vice president and director of the NEC Institute of Management. Costs are effectively amortized by the benefit gained from more productive employees over their entire work life with the company.

- *Fuji Xerox.* Cultural changes are putting pressure on the so-called lifetime employment system. Takuo Kawaguchi, manager of the personnel division for Fuji Xerox, observes that "traditional personnel management in Japan has been based on long-term benefits. This orientation is not entirely compatible with the increasing desires of younger people to secure quick rewards." These changes are leading to a rise in job-hopping behavior, and, consequently, may lead some Japanese firms to moderate their extensive employee educational efforts. However, most leading Japanese companies will probably continue to stress the importance of executive and staff training, while trying to encourage employees to remain loyal through improvements in the quality of work life and greater attention to the development of career paths for promising young executives.

Advanced Management-Training Courses

Although training is often associated with lower-level management development, more and more companies are continuing to develop senior managers through advanced management courses. The rapid pace of change in management practices is a strong reason for companies to train their senior managers. In addition, a prestigious advanced management-training course can serve as a reward for senior executives, as well as provide them with an occasion to interact with other top executives. When the training is conducted outside the company, it can prove a good opportunity for cross-fertilization as executives learn about new methods used at other companies. Another reason to provide top executives with advanced management training is that upper-level managers typically serve longer in each assignment than midlevel managers. Advanced courses offer exposure to a variety of people and ideas that greater mobility would otherwise provide.

For senior managers—whether expatriates, TCNs or LNs—training often takes place outside the company. The main reason for this is that by the time executives reach the highest management echelons, there may be little left for the company to teach them. Although some companies handle advanced management training internally, such programs require significant financial and logistical resources. After all, to justify the expenditure of senior executives' time, the quality of the training must be exceptional.

External Programs.   For the majority of companies that send top executives outside, the type of training chosen is most often a short-term program at a major graduate business school.

- *Colgate-Palmolive* has purposely reduced senior executive mobility in recent years as part of a general corporate plan to improve continuity and accountability in a given business. "Whereas 10 years ago it was not uncommon for a general manager to move to a new subsidiary every two or three years, that's almost never done now," says director of management and organization development Whitaker. As a result, "the opportunity to learn by getting new jobs frequently isn't there anymore." Moreover, as the company changes—adopts new technologies, increases cross-functional responsibilities and otherwise adapts to the times—older executives have to keep pace and can thus benefit from training.

  For these reasons, the company sends senior executives to various advanced management programs at leading business schools such as Harvard, Stanford, Wharton, Insead, Darden and the Asian Institute of Management in the Philippines. "We are looking for programs that, first of all, teach business strategy and will help our people develop into strategic thinkers. Second, we want the program to have a global focus," says Colgate-Palmolive's Whitaker.

  Another objective is to ensure that the training programs bring together people from many different environments. "We want them to be studying global issues and global companies, so we like to see that the peer group in the program is multinational. We don't want

Europeans studying with Europeans, or Americans with Americans." According to Whitaker, Colgate's goal is that every manager enrolled in an external program return with a fresh perspective. "We want them to literally get out of the Colgate box," she says.

Colgate-Palmolive currently sends employees to outside programs, because its own "current resources internally are rather lean." In the future, it plans to expand its internal resources, in particular in the interpersonal and managing-people areas, which the company has found are best taught internally.

- *Fuji Xerox* frequently sends senior managers to summer executive programs held by The Wharton Business School of the University of Pennsylvania and the University of California at Los Angeles (UCLA).

Alternatively, companies often develop a curriculum with a business school. For example, Digital Equipment has developed relationships with Insead in Fontainebleau, Templeton College, Oxford and IMD in Lausanne. Most MNCs send executives to advanced management programs at one time or another. Companies that have recently sent senior managers to Columbia University's Graduate School of Business include Exxon, BASF, IBM and Rolls-Royce; some recent subscribers to programs at Insead are AT&T, BASF, British Petroleum, IBM and Sandoz; and Harvard clients have included AT&T, General Motors, Mitsui, Rank Xerox, Shell and Westinghouse. (See Appendix for a list of select advanced management programs.)

Internal Programs. Companies that do their own senior-level training tend to be large MNCs with a strong training tradition, such as IBM and Philips.

- *IBM* offers two programs for senior executives: the 10-day executive seminar for experienced executives (those with three to five years in significant jobs) and the prestigious International Executive Program (IEP). The IEP is limited to about 10 very senior people, usually drawn from the ranks of country general managers and heads of major functions. The CEO handpicks participants from a list of candidates provided by the corporate international human resources department.

- *Philips* also provides a variety of developmental programs for senior managers. The most important is a three-week senior international program for about 60 executives per year. Also, the compa-

Types of International Education Courses,
NEC Institute of Management,
Tokyo, Japan

Main Category	Topics
1. International Communication (21 separate courses)	English Conversation English Composition English Presentations Cross-Cultural Communication Other Foreign Languages Linguistic Ability Diagnosis
2. International Management	International Senior Manager Course International Middle Manager Course International Operations Case Studies Seminar
3. International Business	Trade Practices Course Advanced Trade Practices Course International Finance Course International Insurance Course International Legal Affairs Contracts Course International Operations Accounting Course International Marketing Course Overseas Project Planning Course International Production Course
4. Area Studies	North American Business Course US EEO (Equal Employment Opportunity) Course European Business Course Asian Business Course Middle-Near East Business Course Central-South American Business Course Oceania Business Course
5. Preparatory to Departure for Overseas Assignment	Predeparture Course Spouses' Course
6. During Overseas Assignment	Overseas Assignees Correspondence Course
7. Postrepatriation	Course for Returned Overseas Assignees

(Continued)

Types of International Education Courses,
NEC Institute of Management,
Tokyo, Japan

Main Category	Topics
8. Overseas Study (Administered by NEC Corporate Human Resources Development Department)	Overseas Study Long Term Short Term (Business Courses) Study in Japan (Two Years)
9. Overseas Business Training (Same as 8)	Long-Term (Two Years) Assignment at Overseas Location for On-the-Job Development
10. Overseas Training for Technicians	Overseas Trip for Further Training
11. Divisional International Education	Overseas Business Group Personnel Group—International Personnel Training
12. Locally Recruited Staff	NEC Overseas Managers' Program Correspondence Courses for Locally Recruited Staff NEC Management News

ny insists that executives attend refresher courses in management
issues and techniques.

- *Bull* offers three types of internal training programs for senior executives. The first, which lasts one to two days, typically covers general policy and strategy. The second consists of more intensive and
focused sessions, and lasts three days to a week. The issues
addressed often relate to specific management problems, e.g., helping workers adjust to change.

    The final segment is an international program for newly appoint-
ed managers, which concentrates on global strategy and economic
or political issues the company faces in the years ahead. Offered
once a year to between 16 and 20 executives, the training program
lasts four to five weeks and requires participants to travel to company locations in Europe, North America and Asia. "The program
usually starts in Paris, then moves elsewhere in Europe, before taking off around the world," says a senior manager. "A typical itiner-

ary might take executives from Paris to Bonn to Budapest to Boston to Taiwan."

The curriculum covers three areas: (1) the study of general strategic, economic and political issues; (2) development of a global business point of view; and (3) examination of the relationship between Europe, Asia and North America. Instruction is provided by lecturers from various universities and often includes meetings with government officials and other VIPs. Fifty of Bull's 175 top executives have participated in the program.

Companies need not have a huge training operation to fashion a useful program for senior international managers, however.

- *Coca-Cola* recently put its senior-management teams through a "managing competitive advantage" program. Composed of teams of managers who actually work together in practice, the three-and-a-half-day program was designed to let them tackle real problems in a training context. By providing them with a planning process for working through a problem from real life, the program not only provided training, but accomplished practical goals as well.

Training Local Nationals

As more companies rely on LNs to staff foreign management posts, instruction geared to their needs is becoming an increasing part of the training effort. For example, to provide its LNs with useful business insights about the US, *AT&T* offers a course at its Brussels center on "doing business in America." In fact, a growing percentage of AT&T's training budget is devoted to adapting this kind of standard course material to serve the particular perspective of LNs.

- *AT&T's approach.* Recently, for example, AT&T exported one course, its "Business Directions Series" (BDS), from the US to regional training centers in Brussels and Singapore. Designed for first- and second-level managers, BDS covers AT&T's overall corporate strategy, strategic direction and key elements of its management philosophy. It consists of videotapes of presentations by CEO Bob Allen, motivational videotapes and various other management-development materials. The course is offered when sufficient need in either region is demonstrated.

Exporting the course, however, required a number of adjustments. The company tested reaction to the course by bringing LN

Teaching in One Language or Many?

A common problem for MNCs that conduct extensive training programs for their LN managers is choosing the language (or languages) in which the courses will be taught. Some companies use only the language of the corporation's home country; others provide instruction in local languages as well.

Generally, the higher the level of the executives who receive training, the more likely it is that the classes will be conducted in the home-country language. Lower-level managers are likely to benefit most from instruction provided in their own language. One way to increase the available audience for a given training package is to design the course in English—probably the most widely spoken language today. Both Bull and Philips, for example, offer training courses in English. Since relatively few people outside Japan have yet to master Japanese, Matsushita has vastly increased the level of access to its programs by preparing its training materials in Japanese, English, Spanish and German.

office managers from different countries to the US to participate. "I happened to sit through the final debriefing day and realized there were some messages that needed to be clarified if they were going to get through to our people overseas," says AT&T's Burgas. "For instance, there were some team-building exercises that we decided would be inappropriate for our Asian employees—a lot of `touchy-feely' stuff that we realized wouldn't go over too well in Asia. These included one exercise in which people become entwined while holding a rope and then work together to get out of this `knotty' situation."

AT&T replaced this rope game with a verbal exercise. "That was what we meant by `internationalizing' the program," Burgas says. "We discovered that we had assumed everyone would know what we meant by *team building*. Certainly, we Americans understand it. But it was clear after one session with our foreign managers that there is a great deal of difference between what a German means by team building and how a Japanese understands the concept." The international version of BDS now contains a careful explanation and discussion of the AT&T notion of team building so that participants do not go through the course with their own individual definitions in mind.

AT&T also offers numerous courses for LNs abroad on a regular basis at its training centers in Brussels and Singapore. Twice annually, the Brussels center publishes a list of courses that includes information on necessary prerequisites, intended audience and the length, description, goals and dates of the course. Courses range in length from two days for management-type courses to much longer for technical-support training. Strategic business negotiating, accomplishments through team work, an introduction to the UNIX computer operating system and shell programming are typical course titles. Because courses given in Brussels are offered to executives all over Europe, the curriculum, if not explicitly international, must be designed to appeal to a multinational audience.

In addition to offering courses abroad, AT&T makes courses offered in the US available to LNs. "If there is a specific course not listed in Brussels or Singapore, and the foreign manager can demonstrate a need for that particular type of instruction," says Burgas, "he or she can register for it here in the US." In such a case, while on a trip to the US, the executive might take the course at AT&T's Corporate Education Training facility in Somerset or Hopewell, New Jersey, at one of some 35 other regional training centers elsewhere in the US or at the headquarters of the manager's business unit. To facilitate the process, the company has established special telephone numbers that permit LNs to call directly into their business unit's training department in order to make arrangements to take courses in the US.

■ *Matsushita's approach.* The Matsushita group currently has three large overseas training centers geared primarily to the needs of local nationals, located in Secaucus, New Jersey, in the US, Frankfurt am Main in Germany and Singapore. "These centers are already educating a lot of people in several key functional fields,"says Matsushita's Umeoka. "For example, the US training center has developed a program in accounting."

In addition to technical training, the centers serve as a focus for disseminating the Matsushita business mission and its service philosophy. "The president of the Matsushita group and other top executives from the head office in Osaka visit these centers during their business trips and often use the opportunity to speak to employees about key issues facing the company," says Umeoka.

Regional training programs occasionally develop their own areas of focus. In North America, Matsushita Electric Corp of America (MECA)'s training effort now emphasizes the education of top executives. In Singapore, the principal objective is to help midlevel employees improve manufacturing, engineering and other technical skills. The effort in Frankfurt aims at upgrading sales and marketing capabilities.

To supplement the in-country training LNs receive, NEC often brings them to Tokyo for a one-month "overseas management program." According to NEC's Hasegawa, "The first part features a common program for all participants"; it is designed to deepen understanding of NEC's management philosophy and its various business activities. The remaining week is devoted to "an individualized program based on each trainee's functions and responsibilities," including on-the-job training with the LN's related functional division (say, manufacturing or finance). Besides enhancing the LN's practical knowledge, this part of the program helps promote better personal relations within the company through interaction and exchange with Japanese staff. About 20 foreign executives at a time participate in this program, which is held three to four times a year.

- *IBM* also offers all executives, including LNs, basic management training at its "New Manager School." A week in duration, the course covers IBM culture and basic beliefs, as well as such personnel topics as employee appraisals, performance planning, salary administration, compensation practices, equal opportunity and fundamental management skills. According to IBM's Laidlaw, the same material is taught worldwide, "so that all managers have an understanding of the culture, experiences and the very basic precepts of our business."

Special Training for Local Nationals: Eastern Europe

In newly opening markets or less-developed countries, finding qualified local nationals may be more difficult than usual. In Eastern Europe, for example, one human resources executive of a large MNC was recently quoted as saying, "We have two choices, hiring former communists or hiring current ones." Indeed, when it comes to hiring local talent in formerly socialist countries, most firms are hiring former managers at state-run enterprises. Although future university graduates may begin their working lives with more of a market orientation, the majority of potential managers today grew up with the old system.

To help familiarize managers with market concepts and Western practices, a number of management schools have arisen in Eastern Europe, some of them virtually overnight and many with the assistance of schools in the West. Typically, the top schools in every country already enjoy considerable prestige, and their graduates are in great demand, not only at state-run enterprises, but also at Western companies looking to expand in this market. Two such schools are currently operating in Budapest:

- *International Management Center* (IMC). Founded in 1988, the IMC has already graduated a number of classes, offered many short-term seminars and become an integral part of the local business scene. Organized with Western help, its goal is to produce managers for Hungary's transformation from a state-run economy to one organized more along market concepts, according to Zsuzsanna Ranki, the center's managing director. A high percentage of graduates of its 10-month program are accepted at business programs in the US, where they can receive an MBA.

The IMC's curriculum is overseen by the University of Pittsburgh. Thus, graduates of its Young Manager's Program receive a joint certificate from IMC and the University of Pittsburgh. In turn, of 28 graduates in 1989, 10 received scholarships to the University of Pittsburgh; upon completion of four months of study there, they will receive an MBA. Another five received scholarships to Tulane University in New Orleans, Louisiana.

The cost of the program, though reasonable by Western standards, remains very high by local ones. The result is that students cannot afford it themselves. Most students come from state-run companies. The average age of those completing the 10-month program is 31. The curriculum is entirely in English.

In addition to offering its full 10-month program, the school runs numerous three-to-five-day seminars for middle- and senior-level executives. To date, it has put some 800 executives, aged 40-45 on average, through a variety of seminars. Courses are given in English, but translation is often provided.

Typical subjects are finance for financial directors, how to value assets, privatization and new forms of ownership and how to motivate your subordinates.

As the school's reputation has grown, the IMC's Ranki is often called on by headhunters and hiring managers to recommend graduates for jobs at Western companies. Similarly, although most of the company's work has been with state-run firms thus far, as a market economy develops, Ranki expects to do more training for Western companies as well.

■ *International Training Center for Bankers Ltd.* This center, 97%-owned by the Hungarian government and started in 1987, with 3% foreign participation, offers specialized training for Hungarian bankers. While in its first three years it trained an average of about 800 participants a year, in 1990 it taught about 2,000 students, reflecting its rapid growth, says managing director Erszebet Konczol. Most students are between the ages of 30 and 40. Courses typically last two weeks and are paid for by the state companies. Although the primary market for its courses thus far has been the new state-owned commercial banks, some international banks with Hungarian subsidiaries, e.g., the Central European Bank, have put students through different courses. In the future, as firms continue to go private and Western banks enter Hungary, the center expects to train more employees from private firms. Meanwhile, it is helping to build up the level of market-oriented skills among banking managers in Hungary.

5

Developing the International Manager of Tomorrow

Executive Summary

Management training is rarely designed solely to develop technical expertise. An important secondary function of training programs is to help companies track performance and single out managers who have the highest career-growth potential. Increasingly, MNCs are incorporating international experience or even full-length global-development assignments into their management-development programs for high-potential employees, reflecting the growing importance of international markets. As the competition for qualified executives intensifies, a well-run training program will not only spell the difference between retaining talent and losing it, but will also help determine the quality and values of employees who make it to the top.

One of the most important functions of any successful corporation is to prepare its next generation of top executives. All companies, whether multinational or not, try to identify their most promising managers, allocate significant training and other resources to such people and promote them to ever more challenging and responsible positions. To develop tomorrow's global managers, MNCs do the same thing but with an added dimension: They must ensure that these managers gain both domestic and international experience in the early and middle years of their careers.

Programs for High Potentials

Most MNCs create global executives by adopting formal management-development programs aimed at younger executives who are deemed to have "high potential" (often called "high potentials"). Although the meaning of high potential varies by company, assessments are usually based on: (1) the firm's needs, as defined by business lines and strategic goals, (2) external market conditions and (3) employee identification with the value system set by top management. These three factors can come together in a variety of ways. *Philips,* for example, defines high potentials simply as employees with the ability to grow one or two levels. That designation takes into account their distinctive qualities in relation to company needs.

Differing company philosophies regarding what makes a good manager can also affect the way a high-potential program is structured. For example, some companies seek to promote talent by encouraging innovation and risk taking, whereas others require executives to demonstrate predictability and steady performance. The goal that all high-potential programs share, however, is to endow high potentials with a sense of participation in a shared destiny with the company, which will ultimately lead to their assumption of key positions in the corporate hierarchy.

The most important function of a high-potential program is to expose talented employees to important strategic and international issues. This helps high potentials to focus on company growth areas. "Future leaders have to understand where the company is going," explains Bibiana Santiago, *AT&T's* human resources director for Europe, the Middle East and Africa. "Sometimes there are bright individuals who are specializing in the wrong field, a field that for whatever reason the company has decided to leave." To give them a chance to change their own directions, the company advises high potentials of its plans. "In our high-potential program, there is a very close relationship between where the company is going and what type of talent we require to get there," says

Santiago. "This means not just managerial leadership styles, but also the business skills and credentials we need our executives to have."

Company training programs for high potentials can serve other purposes: (1) to create a genuine cadre of well-trained international executives with shared values and experiences, (2) to inspire constructive competition among executives, (3) to draw recruits from outside the company and (4) to demonstrate to employees the company's international commitment. In a very real sense, international training programs can help top management "globalize" a company from below.

The specific elements of programs for high potentials vary, but they typically encompass a range of training courses, one or more "development" assignments abroad and, in the case of foreign nationals tapped for the program, development assignments at the parent company's headquarters.

Pros and Cons of a Formal Program

The chief advantage of a program for high potentials is that it usually spurs the company to do more to develop the employee than it might do otherwise. A formal program clears the way for expenditures of money, clarifies who will receive it and facilitates contact between chosen employees and senior management—a vital aspect of any high-potential effort. "We want to be clear at the corporate senior-management level about who we're going to invest in," says R. Alicia Whitaker, Colgate-Palmolive's director of management and organizational development. "By `invest,' I mean paying for very high-tech, expensive, outside education programs."

The primary disadvantage of a formal program is that it introduces rigidity and an element of bureaucracy into the process. This may cause management to spend too much time and effort on the wrong employees or alternatively, to neglect a talented individual who for some reason has not made the cut. The best defense against this problem is to set up thorough and regular review systems to ensure that the right people receive the advantages that come from being a high potential.

Examples of High-Potential Programs

- *Colgate-Palmolive* begins creating its global managers at the start of their careers, drawing participants directly from college or business school (see box below). Not only does the company gain a head start on its global competitors, but it also creates a corps of future international leaders. Although its program does not spur internal competition—since all recruits come directly from school—its selectivity and comprehensiveness have made Colgate a highly attractive employer to many students. The company is able to choose top graduates, thus raising the quality level of its managerial work force.

Colgate-Palmolive: Creating Tomorrow's Global Marketing Managers

The goal of Colgate-Palmolive's global marketing training program is an ambitious one: to create a cadre of managers with a commitment to leadership in the global markets of the future. As a consumer products company, Colgate Palmolive depends heavily on the effectiveness of its marketing and the quality of its marketing personnel. Moreover, with non-US revenues accounting for more than 65% of sales, international marketing skills are one of the company's vital strategic resources.

Founded in 1986, the two-year global marketing training program is now a corporate institution, and admittance to the program is highly competitive. Each year the company recruits around 20 promising young people for the program—half have just graduated from college, and half are newly minted MBAs. The universe of schools is limited to just 12 US institutions, which include Columbia, Harvard, New York University and Florida A&M University. To select its 20 participants, Colgate generally interviews about 120 young people, who themselves have been winnowed from a much larger group of candidates.

Colgate seeks individuals with leadership capabilities, the ability to speak at least one foreign language and exposure to an international environment. For US citizens, this often means having lived overseas (perhaps because a parent worked for an MNC or was in the diplomatic corps or the armed forces) or studied abroad while in college. The company has been quite successful in hiring non-US students who speak English and several other languages.

Once chosen, the young hires receive training in everything from computer programming to sales. Typically, out of the two years in the program, seven months are spent in direct sales. "We take these very bright individuals and don't just have them follow a salesperson around for a day," says Colgate's Whitaker. "They become Colgate salespeople and develop relationships that, in some cases, will last through their entire careers in the company." Although the program's two years are generally spent in the US, the training involves enough international material so that at the end of the program, trainees are expected to be ready to assume positions abroad. Typically, about half the participants go abroad when they complete the course. These postings usually last three to five years.

A distinct characteristic of the global marketing training program is that each trainee is assigned a more experienced manager as a mentor to help ease the way through the early years in the company. Although Colgate has great confidence in its trainees, it requires them to continue to prove themselves. "We've taken the position that we're only going to send excellent people abroad," says Whitaker. "We have very rigorous standards in our global training program and we fire people who are not performing well. We strongly resist the idea of exporting people who are not going to be high-quality producers."

- *Philips* also has developed an innovative way to cultivate young managers who have an interest in international service. Philips has created the Octagon Program (see box p. 104) to help identify the best of its high-potential junior executives. (The program is called *Octagon*, because it groups three teams of eight executives in an annual test of ingenuity.) Like Colgate-Palmolive, Philips uses the program to introduce high potentials to senior managers. Promoting interchange between the junior and senior levels serves the company well, for the younger employees can learn a great deal from senior managers, who, in turn, can get to know the up-and-coming leaders and make maximum use of their talents.

- *Mitsui & Co*, the giant Japanese general trading company, is another MNC with a long-standing (pre-World War II) training program for younger international executives. According to the *Report of the Research Committee on International Executive Education* (published by the Tokyo-based Japan Overseas Enterprise Association in May 1989), the program was discontinued during the war, but revived in 1952. At that time, four trainees a year were sent to the US or the UK.

At present, about 20 trainees participate in the program year-

Philips: The Octagon Program

Philips annually selects 24 of its European high potentials—mostly between ages 32 and 35—to participate in its prestigious Octagon Program, a test of individual and small-group problem-solving abilities. The 24 enrollees are divided into three groups of eight, and the groups are given a complicated problem to resolve, using a combination of individual initiative and teamwork.

Each year's problem is devised by one of Philips' five top executives. It may center on internal issues, such as the future role of the product manager, or external ones, such as the best way to develop the company's business in Eastern Europe. The program lasts about three months and takes place outside normal working hours.

There is no guidance from other company executives, but members are encouraged to interview anyone they wish, both inside and outside the company. Each team subdivides its major tasks so that every participant has individual, as well as collective, responsibility for identifying the appropriate issues, devising a solution and formulating a plan to implement it.

At the end of three months, the various groups have to integrate their findings in the form of a well-written report and present their recommendations to a panel consisting of top executives. Depending on the quality of the recommendations and the discussion, the Board of Management may decide to distribute the report to senior management in the company for serious consideration or even to adopt certain recommendations as policy guidelines.

Though the Octagon exercise is currently offered only to European executives, Philips is examining the feasibility of introducing a similar program for young managers in the US and in Asia.

ly, and the list of host countries has grown to include France, Germany, Italy, Spain, Portugal, China, Indonesia, Thailand, Iran and various Arab states, in addition to the UK and the US. Each trainee spends one year at a business or language school, followed by a year or more of practical work experience. As of 1988, 737 Mitsui executives had participated. After successfully completing this program, individuals are eligible for additional training, which lasts three months to a year and concentrates on a specific business area (e.g., retail marketing) or on work that leads to an advanced degree.

- *IBM* has a shorter-term approach to training newly appointed executives or high-potential individuals from various parts of the world. It offers 20 of these individuals at a time a two-week program on international issues at one of six training centers in Armonk, New York and five other locations around the world. Like other such programs, it serves several purposes: (1) to educate, (2) to confer prestige and (3) to bring participants to the attention of senior executives. "In almost every class, senior people meet with the younger managers," says director of executive resources and development Laidlaw. "For instance, at the program here in the US our chairman spends two to four hours with almost every class. In Europe, the president of IBM Europe spends a similar amount of time with the Brussels classes, as do some of our senior country executives. The same is true in Asia. And, of course, the diverse participants learn from one another as well." Laidlaw says that the thrust of the courses is primarily external "to give these new managers an understanding of global interaction, of global economies, of global politics."

- *Fuji Xerox* also offers special tours abroad to promising staff members or managerial candidates. Given the company's close ties to Xerox in the US and Rank Xerox in Europe, Fuji Xerox has long emphasized cross-cultural education. For the past 17 years, the firm has sent a select group of promising young staff members abroad for training in either the US or Europe. While some of the trainees sent to the US complete a two-year MBA at prestigious schools like Harvard, Wharton and MIT, others spend one year at a university and one year on the job in a relevant Xerox unit. Hideki Kaihatsu, a Fuji Xerox director and the company's former senior resident at Xerox headquarters in Stamford, Connecticut, believes that the latter option is preferable, because it permits young Japanese managers to gain postgraduate experience and become acquainted with a wide range of people at Xerox.

  More recently, the firm has expanded the program to its five Asian affiliates (in South Korea, Taiwan, Indonesia, the Philippines and Thailand), where the young Japanese staff members learn about operations and, of course, business practices, social conditions and culture in these countries. Participants typically spend the first year at a language school and become familiar with local culture and daily life. The second year is devoted to on-the-job training at the local Fuji Xerox affiliate.

For a number of years, the Fuji Xerox Learning Institute in Tokyo has offered an intercultural communication program aimed at helping non-Japanese communicate more effectively with their Japanese counterparts. The program is similar to the Internationalized Education Program (discussed in Chapter 2) designed for the firm's Japanese employees, but is also available to individuals who are not employees of Xerox Corp or Fuji Xerox. At present, Fuji Xerox has about three American employees, in addition to about 20 expatriates on assignment from Brazil, Canada, the UK and the US.

Last year, the Tokyo-based joint-venture firm selected five people for training in the US and a second complement of five staff members for two-year terms in Asian countries. In choosing among candidates, "we look for people with open minds who can cope with living abroad, who can work together with people of different cultures, who have a good track record at work and who have the potential to make a strong contribution to the company when they return," says Masahiro Haraguchi, deputy manager of the firm's management and resources development center. Besides using subjective evaluations, the company puts candidates through a battery of tests to measure language ability, interpersonal skills, management aptitude and the ability to manage stress.

Fuji Xerox provides selected candidates with six months of pre-departure training before they go overseas. Although departing expatriates continue to work in their departments during the first three months, they study full time during the latter three months. Much of the training they receive is in the language of the destination country. "Every day for three months for four hours a day" they receive language training, explains Takuo Kawaguchi, manager of Fuji Xerox's personnel division. In addition to an intensive language course, departing expatriates are schooled in such topics as how to obtain visas, find places to live and the nature of their new jobs.

Employees participating in the US or UK training programs should not expect to receive automatic raises in salary or other benefits once they receive MBAs, notes Haraguchi. "However, with the two years of experience abroad, they have added knowledge that comes out in their work performance and could be considered an advantage for the future."

Haraguchi acknowledges that one of the problems with this policy is that a few former participants have left the company, eager to capitalize on their enhanced earning power. "In the face of the fast pace of globalization, people just don't follow the old rules," adds

Kawaguchi. To keep up with cultural changes in Japan that encourage more job-hopping among employees, Fuji Xerox has begun to query potential candidates about their plans before sending them abroad and is launching other programs to improve the work atmosphere and career prospects for Fuji Xerox employees. For the time being, however, the company remains quite satisfied with the cost/reward benefits of its current program.

Choosing High Potentials

At most MNCs, high potentials are proposed by their immediate supervisors and then screened by a committee composed of senior managers from the country operation where the person works and representatives of the parent company's personnel department.

- *Philips'* review committees, for example, consist of the CEO of the country affiliate or the chairman of the product division, the local human resources director and personnel executives from headquarters. "Each product division has a human resources director who is present in the discussion, in addition to myself or someone else from the corporate department," says managing director of the corporate staff bureau J. D. de Leeuw.

   The committee discussions are based on formal preparatory evaluation at decentralized levels in the product divisions of national organizations. As a basis for judging the growth potential of a person, a company potential appraisal system may be used, which contains criteria that are seen as relevant and indicative of future career success. Candidates are evaluated for high-potential status each year, and the progress of those already designated as high potentials is also reviewed annually to determine whether they should remain on the list. Thus, although a candidate may make it onto the list one year, there is no guarantee the designation will be renewed.

   "We review each person again and again to see how he or she performs," says de Leeuw. "It might very well be that after two or three years, the person has reached his or her highest potential, and we decide to add somebody else to the list instead. It's a dynamic process."

- *Rank Xerox* also reassigns high potentials to the list on an annual basis, or drops them. Initially, the assessment is conducted by the person's immediate supervisor. As these executives move into positions of greater visibility, however, the executive management group discusses such issues as their career, training and experience.

- *AT&T* employees must meet a number of criteria to be selected for participation in the company's leadership continuity program (LCP). "One quality we value is for a person to have had international experience or been exposed to our international businesses," says AT&T's Santiago. Other criteria include business results, interpersonal skills, a results orientation and the ability to influence others.

     Candidates are proposed by a sponsoring manager, who is asked to justify the nomination based on the selection criteria. "Each candidate is scrutinized in round table discussions in the business unit, with the level of participants depending on the rank and seniority of the candidate," says Santiago. "If the candidate is in high middle management, this person may have the potential to serve, at some point, as a corporate officer. So that person will probably be reviewed directly by the presidents of the business divisions. High potentials are generally evaluated twice annually and can be added on or dropped."

     AT&T includes 2-5% of its managerial population in the leadership continuity program. Participants are drawn from all areas of the company and include lower, middle and upper-middle management employees.

It is worth noting that companies often continue to use the high-potential designation even when employees reach fairly high levels in the company. "Our system applies to all levels, so you can be on the high-potential list as a general manager or as a product manager," says Henri C. Debuisser, executive director of personnel, organization and corporate affairs at Rank Xerox. He points out, however, that "executives at higher levels have normally translated their potential into accomplishment. They still have high potential, but they are also known to top management for what they have achieved." A Bull human resources manager concurs, noting that after a certain point in their careers, his company's high potentials "are followed case by case, individual by individual, because they now have important jobs."

Should Employees Know?

Only a few companies explicitly tell employees they have been designated as high potentials. Most companies keep this information secret, although some put a special code on the computerized personnel files of high-potential designees. The advantage of informing people of their status is that they have an incentive to perform at their maximum levels at all times. The disadvantages are that the chosen executives may become complacent or smug and that valued employees not selected may "give up" and perform suboptimally.

- *Rank Xerox* is one of the many MNCs that keeps its list of high potentials confidential. Bull does not formally notify employees that they have been designated as high potentials, but employees know anyway. "They get feedback from their managers, and they have annual performance reviews," explains a Bull senior executive. "Some are given more and faster job changes and promotions than their peers. These employees know they are on a faster track."

- *AT&T*, in contrast, informs employees as to whether or not they are high potentials. "It's secretive in the sense that there is no master list, but the employee is personally made aware of his or her status," says Santiago. This policy is consistent with AT&T's belief that career management is a three-tiered responsibility, which involves the company, the supervisor and the employee. "If an employee has responsibility for his or her own career development, then it follows that he or she should know whether they're LCP [Leadership Continuity Program] or not," says Santiago. "They also have a right to understand how we define LCP and what they need to do to obtain that status."

- *Philips* leaves the matter of whether or not to tell an executive to each department head's discretion. "Officially, there is no rule on this," says de Leeuw. "The decision depends on the culture of the department and how keen the individual is to know his potential."

The Global-Development Assignment

Participation in high-potential programs is not always synonymous with extensive exposure to international business, even in companies with a global network of operations. At *IBM*, a highly internationalized manufacturer, only a third of high-potential candidates actually serve outside their home country. Indeed, according to a recent survey by consultants Moran, Stahl & Boyer (MS&B), only about 35% of major US companies insist on international assignments as part of their career-planning systems. The survey concluded that a lack of international exposure puts companies at a significant disadvantage in the struggle for global market share.

Who Goes Abroad. Nevertheless, many companies do make a strong effort to single out managers with the skills and talents to succeed internationally as early as possible in their careers. "We have a strategy to develop people as global managers, chiefly by identifying prospects early in their careers and by trying to give them a mix of headquarters and international experiences," says *IBM*'s Laidlaw.

Well before a new crop of global executives is needed, farsighted corporations are preparing those individuals. "My concern is not so much about this year," says Laidlaw. "The fact is we were concerned about creating this year's international managers back in 1985 or earlier. Today, I'm focusing on the year 2000. If we don't identify, develop and train those people today, they won't be available when we need them."

Few firms place their youngest managers in international development assignments; a notable exception is *Colgate-Palmolive* (see box pp. 102–103). Instead, most place middle-management executives abroad. A high potential sent overseas should be at least a "second-level manager," says Laidlaw. "Second-level managers at IBM generally have been with the company from six to 11 years and have other managers reporting to them. Our experience has been that if people go out into the field much before then, they're really not high enough in the organization to get maximum exposure and visibility. What happens is that they're just doing work in another country, but are not gaining the managerial and cross-cultural experience they should have."

However, assuming managers have reached this level, deploying them abroad represents a good way to develop their talents. Of *IBM's* approximately 3,000 expatriates, one third have been sent out specifically to give them international experience. The others are dispatched to an overseas subsidiary for another primary reason—either to assist with a product transfer or to learn a critical skill not available in their home countries—but they, of course, gain international savvy as well. "At some point in the career of a high potential, we try to identify an appropriate assignment in another part of the world," says Laidlaw. "This holds true not only for US nationals, but for our high-potential people from Germany, France, the UK, Japan—all of our largest affiliates."

Although IBM tries to offer high-potential individuals the opportunity to serve abroad, "there just aren't enough international assignments to go around," says Laidlaw. Moreover, the company tries to match the needs of the employee with those of the business. Finally, it must keep an eye on the bottom line. "When people go on a foreign assignment, by the time we count the allowances and everything else involved, we really have to make sure there's a payback to the company," he says.

Dow Chemical is another company that uses global-development assignments to provide promising executives with international experience. Indeed, because of the expense involved, the company rarely moves junior executives who are not identified as having high potential. "If you want to move someone who hasn't been identified as in need of a move for development, you have to explain that to top management," says Peter J. Cohen, director of human resources and administrative services for Dow Chemical Japan. Indeed, although the company recognizes that experience gained in Japan can be quite valuable, the high costs preclude Tokyo's use as a common training ground for young expatriates. "There are places where it makes sense to send a person out for some experience, but this is not one of them," says Cohen.

The Most Suitable Jobs.   What are the best international jobs for a young high-potential manager? Philips identifies appropriate postings on a systematic basis as part of its program. "Our high potentials in their early 30s are usually well suited for a management function in a small plant," says de Leeuw. "We can also give the person a product marketing function in a larger national organization or the position of general manager in a small national organization."

Although the range of positions used as development assignments varies widely, sales and marketing jobs are among the most frequently chosen. Such positions offer young employees broad exposure to the foreign environment and require them to interact with customers, distributors and service organizations (such as market research houses, advertising agencies and public relations firms) and to speak the local language.

Bringing Promising Executive Talent From the Field

In addition to training designed to help those going out into the field, a few companies have programs to train people, usually LNs, brought from the field to headquarters.

- *IBM,* for example, has a program that brings young mid-level foreign executives to corporate headquarters where they commonly serve as administrative assistants in the chairman's office. In addition, IBM often assigns non-US nationals to areas other than their country of origin as part of the firm's management-development program. In particular, it may bring executives to regional headquarters.

- *Dow Chemical Japan.* Dow Chemical Japan also makes a practice of "identifying local nationals who would benefit from an overseas posting, as well as giving consideration to where to send them," says Cohen. Indeed, Dow's US business units are eager to receive Japanese sales staffers to sell to Japanese clients in the US (see box p. 112).

Dow Chemical: Using Japanese Expatriate Sales Staff for Overseas Japanese Clients

As Japanese companies have enlarged their presence in the US, they have often become significant customers of US companies. Some US companies, such as Dow Chemical, have found that their Japanese corporate customers respond best to sales representatives from their own country. As a result, Dow's Peter J. Cohen reports that "many of our US strategic business units (SBUs) are asking us to send Japanese nationals to their organizations to act as liaisons and sales managers for their Japanese clients." Thanks to the rapid action of Dow's Japanese subsidiary to fill this demand, "the US sales numbers are benefiting," reports Cohen. Moreover, he notes that this trend also happens to "provide an excellent opportunity for the development of some of our younger people."

The ability of Dow Chemical's Japanese sales executives to forge closer relationships with buyers at US subsidiaries of Japanese MNCs may be particularly useful now, as many of Dow's corporate global client relationships are being increasingly managed by its smaller, specialized SBUs. For example, Cohen relates, "Various companies in Japan supply raw materials to some of our US facilities. Although the purchases of these materials may not be huge in monetary terms, they are vital to the continued operation of those plants in the US. We have to establish good ties with the Japanese suppliers here and manage these relationships both from Tokyo and Midland. This need provides useful opportunities for our local employees to get involved in global business."

Dow Chemical Japan has about 17 Japanese employees out of 500 working abroad; most are in the US, but some are assigned to Hong Kong and Europe. Says Cohen, "The same process is beginning to occur in Europe. Japanese subsidiaries, particularly in automotives and electronics, are starting to require the same type of service as in the US. Our European subs are already asking us for Japanese staffers to go over and help fill this need."

- *MEI* recently began hiring some foreign executives directly out of college. In turn, it has brought a few of them to headquarters to experience the Matsushita group's core culture firsthand. "This year, between seven and 10 people will be coming here from abroad to work in Japan after being directly recruited from college," says Nobuo Umeoka, assistant general manager for corporate personnel at MEI's Osaka headquarters.

  MEI is also bringing an increasing number of local middle managers from its offshore affiliates to Osaka for programs, extending from three months to a year, which involve study at Matsushita's Overseas Training Center at Hirakata (near Osaka) and work in various departments, ranging from manufacturing and product development to marketing and administration. Says Umeoka, "We would like local nationals in our affiliates to know about the decision-making process and working systems here in Matsushita and to get to know executive class people here who really have the authority to make major decisions."

- *Fuji Xerox* regularly brings five promising young executives, one from each of its five Asian affiliates, to Japanese headquarters for a two-year management-training program. More than a decade old, this program is the mirror image of the company's plan for sending young Japanese staffers overseas as described above. Participants, who are usually at the department head (or *bu-cho*) level, study the Japanese language, management and culture during the first year and spend the second year engaged in on-the-job training "in the department of their choice," says Haraguchi. He cites executives from Taiwan as having been particularly successful—management committee meetings at Fuji Xerox's affiliate in Taipei are often conducted in Japanese. Executives usually bring their families to Japan as well. To ensure a smooth adjustment, Fuji Xerox arranges for housing and schooling of the children and provides orientation for both the executive and spouse.

Using High Potentials in Succession Planning

Another key ingredient in an international high-potential program is the so-called global replacement table, which lists preferred successors for important positions in the company. Many companies still maintain these lists on paper, but more and more firms have computerized replacement tables as part of an effort to document the succession process on a comprehensive, worldwide basis.

IBM: State-of-the-Art Personnel Tracking

IBM uses an advanced computer program to track potential candidates for the company's 1,600 senior management positions, which includes a range of job titles from country and product managers all the way up to CEO. Each position has a citation that lists the names and current assignments of four potential successors, who are usually identified by the executive responsible for the position. The data are kept strictly confidential and can be assessed only by responsible executive resources personnel. The company has also automated succession planning for lower-level managers, but staffing decisions are normally handled by the country operations.

Candidates are ranked according to criteria that range from suitability to availability to make the move. In addition, the system keeps track of biographical data such as age, previous job history and language skills. Supervisors are responsible for updating names and other data every year.

Despite the high-tech emphasis, Don Laidlaw stresses that a high amount of personal judgment is involved in the actual selection of a successor. "We involve the immediate manager or executive directly in this process, because he or she is most familiar with not only the job requirements, but what characteristics the candidate must have to succeed in the position," he says.

- *IBM* has a particularly advanced computer system to track the movements of key managers in its worldwide operations (see box above).

- *GM's* Electronic Data Systems division developed a computer system to track positions held by management personnel. The system permits corporate human resources to identify at the touch of a button potentially qualified personnel for specific job postings on a worldwide basis. "The system is used primarily in staffing higher-level executive positions for our overseas facilities," says GM's director of international human resources Guerrier.

- *Philips* also has a formal tracking system geared toward succession planning. Responsibility for keeping such lists rests with the product divisions and country affiliates, but procedures are set by international human resources and reviewed periodically. "Once a year, we review the succession plan for key positions in strategically important areas. These include the consumer electronics division, the lighting division and the domestic appliances division, as well as major countries like France, the UK, Germany and the US," says de Leeuw. During these discussions, many candidates are considered. "If you looked at our official succession schemes, you would find everything from no candidates to as many as five," he says. "But in most cases there are two or three."

6
Strategies for Successful Repatriation

Executive Summary

Handling the return of expatriates to headquarters or their continued development overseas is a make-or-break experience for both the employee and the company. For the employee, successful transitions will keep a career on track. For the company, it is key to making the most of the large investment an international executive represents.

To retain top international managers, companies are using methods like mentor programs to ensure that returnees find positions within the organization and global career-pathing techniques to spearhead successful transitions. Today's international manager will often have several international assignments before being posted to headquarters.

By the time international executives reach upper-middle or senior manager status, their employers will have spent enormous sums on them for recruitment, training and support, in addition to salary,incentive compensation and benefits. The total can easily come to hundreds of thousands (if not millions) of dollars per individual. At this point, clearly, an executive should be considered an investment rather than a cost, a part of the firm's human-asset base of accumulated skills and knowledge. Too often, however, companies fail to harvest this expertise in a way that protects their investment.

A Growing Problem

The inability to effectively manage the careers of international executives often results in employee dissatisfaction among those who remain with the company. Others decide to look outside the company for job opportunities. In fact, retention rates for employees sent to positions overseas, which were never high, have fallen significantly since the "downsizing" initiatives of the last decade cut back the scale of headquarters' operations. According to a 1989 survey by Moran, Stahl & Boyer (MS&B), of 56 MNCs studied, 10% have had problems with attrition among repatriated executives.

It is not surprising that many executives are dissatisfied with the repatriation experience. After completing an overseas assignment, some expatriates must wait months for new assignments; sometimes these do not materialize. Others are given posts that rank lower than their previous jobs or that do not allow them to use the skills learned abroad.

The effects of these problems were evident in MS&B's study. The MS&B study found that at over half the firms (56%), foreign assignments are considered either detrimental or immaterial to an executive's career, i.e., unlikely to lead to promotions and career advancement. Only 17% of respondents felt their firm's repatriation policies were "adequate in addressing the needs for career development," while a mere 20% were satisfied with these policies when it came to "meeting the adjustment and reintegration needs of returning expatriates."[1] Given figures like these, it is not surprising that MNCs may find it difficult to persuade their most talented managers to work abroad for an extended period.

To combat the problem, the most globally oriented companies, which are the most vulnerable to a shortage of committed "internationalists," have begun to treat repatriation planning and support as an integral part of the executive-recruitment process. Following are some of the approaches being used:

---

[1]Moran, Stahl & Boyer, 1989, *Repatriation of American Expatriates, Survey Results.*

1. Sponsors or mentors for expatriates and TCNs during their tours abroad
2. Employee-assistance programs (EAPs) for executives based at foreign affiliates
3. Prerepatriation and postrepatriation counseling
4. Predeparture training (i.e., before the executive ever goes overseas), which includes discussions of the manager's ultimate repatriation
5. Written job guarantees

Alternatively, some companies are developing new global career paths geared to expatriates who would rather remain abroad than return home. Instead of bringing talented managers back to marginal jobs at headquarters or a domestic operating unit, companies may cycle managers through many overseas assignments before repatriating them. Indeed, some of today's top executives literally worked their way around the world before returning to a top position at corporate headquarters.

Even a modest effort to improve repatriation can pay large dividends. Simple acknowledgment by management that repatriation problems exist is an important first step. Not only will improved repatriation procedures reduce the incidence of outright failure, they will also create more satisfied executives and enhance their understanding of international issues, which is a prerequisite for any globalization strategy.

Two Key Concerns

Companies frequently confront two critical issues in devising appropriate assignments for executives whose foreign postings are ending. First, there may be no suitable job available at the time the executive returns home. Second, the executive may not adapt well to the environment of his domestic assignment. Difficulties may arise because, for example, domestic operations are usually larger and more structured than those abroad.

Finding a Suitable Job

Unlike a domestic position, an international job usually has a fixed end point. A domestic executive is under no pressure to change jobs by a certain date, but expatriates or TCNs know from the start of an overseas assignment exactly when they are supposed to leave. Thus, unless work on finding new positions begins well in advance, returning managers' options will be limited by what happens to be available when their tours of duty abroad are over.

One result of having this "deadline" hanging over their heads is that executives become anxious about their job prospects. This, in turn, can mean a decline in their effectiveness during the last few months of the foreign posting or, in some cases, much longer. This uncertainty over a new assignment makes the repatriation experience an unpleasant one for the employee.

According to one former US expatriate who was based in London in the mid-1980s: "I started worrying about what I would do when I went back to the US about halfway through my four-year assignment. Since my company did not guarantee me any job, much less a particular job when I returned, my concern turned out to be entirely justified. I ended up in a kind of backwater in the international division, and three years later I left the company."

Executives posted abroad are often not in the best position to mount their own internal job searches. After three or more years abroad, they may have lost touch with old bosses and colleagues. And they probably are not in close communication with people in the corporate personnel department, except perhaps for the manager who handles compensation or benefits for expatriates. Repatriation is often particularly difficult for TCNs, who are unlikely to have had previous experience at headquarters, and consequently, may lack contacts to draw on. Hoping for an assignment in their home country may be futile, especially if their company's operations there are fairly small.

In the extreme case where no job is available, executives, whether originally from the home country or elsewhere, may find themselves effectively furloughed, if not fired. "Most people are basically optimistic," says the international human resources director of one large European MNC. "Before they go abroad, we tell them we don't know what will happen in three years, but their typical response is that other opportunities are bound to come along. They say things like, `If I succeed, I'll be a hero.' But this is not necessarily the case. We may have the idea of making an expatriate a marketing director at home, but if that job becomes available before he comes back, we cannot hold it open. So when he gets home, there's no job."

Despite the problems it poses, the preset term for an overseas assignment is unlikely to be abolished. In the first place, many countries' immigration and employment rules impose fixed time limits on foreign workers. Therefore, as a practical matter, MNCs must remove expatriates and TCNs from foreign postings within a few years. Second, to attract talented employees to international service, a fixed term abroad is usually necessary, lest the assignment appear to be a dead end with no prospects for return.

Adjusting to a New Environment

Even when an executive is given an appropriate job at home, the matter of readjustment is a serious concern. Differences between working abroad and working at headquarters contribute to the adaptation problems many repatriated managers experience. Indeed, coming home after a stint of several years in a foreign country entails the same problems as expatriation, although in reverse.

Cultural differences exist even when a company (e.g., IBM or Coca-Cola) has a consistent culture around the world, and the work environment does not differ much from country to country. "It's the feeling of being a small fish in a big pond when you're back at the home company," says Jim Fisher, *GM*'s staff assistant for international human resources. "Overseas, it's the opposite: Most expatriates are big fish in small ponds."

Companies often expect executives to simply adapt to the change as part of their job. For example, expatriates returning to *Fuji Xerox* offices in Japan must often readjust to a smaller office or house as well as lessened autonomy. Says Masahiro Haraguchi, deputy manager of the firm's Management and Resource Development Center, "Most people are realistic in understanding that life in Japan is not the same as, say, the Philippines, where they can hire domestic help and so forth."

When it comes to less tangible changes, however, such as diminished status, explaining them away is much less simple. The loss of status and perks within the company can take much getting used to for executives weaned on the VIP treatment they received as resident foreigners. In addition, returning executives often chafe at the bureaucratic restrictions of a large headquarters environment, and many feel diminished when they no longer have decision-making autonomy.

Another issue is the adjustment for family members, who may have grown accustomed to a style of living unavailable to them at home, e.g., lavish homes, domestic servants and longer vacations. In addition, children have the problem of adjusting to an unfamiliar home-country school system. Children of Japanese expatriates, in particular, are often ill prepared for the rigorous entrance examinations given by superior senior high schools and top Japanese universities (see "Family Help" below).

Globalization and Repatriation

It should be noted that the severity of both these problems—finding a new job and adjusting to the home environment—varies greatly from company to company and usually relates to the degree of the company's globalization. Problems tend to be least serious at firms with a strong orientation toward doing business abroad. Highly global companies count on their employees' ability to adapt to returning home— just as they count on them to go abroad in the first place. Moving from country to country is, after all, part of the job description.

From the individual employee's perspective, relationships and communication with associates back home are maintained more readily at a global company, because domestic and international activities are not strictly separated, and there is not a "we-they" syndrome. In addition, the average workday of an expatriate involves frequent interaction with the parent company and home-country operating units, which eases the repatriation process. Even more positive is the fact that large, established MNCs value foreign experience and treat their repatriated executives well. Moreover, such firms do not have to look far to find follow-up jobs at home that make use of international experience.

Finally, global corporations are more likely to encourage and provide opportunities for overseas executives to remain abroad, if they so desire, than their more domestically oriented counterparts. *Colgate-Palmolive*, for one, has actually modified its overseas compensation structure so as to make international careers more attractive.

In contrast, the difficulties are often magnified at less global companies. Operations at foreign affiliates often differ significantly from those in the home market, and in many cases, international activities are carried out quite separately from domestic ones. It is not unusual for returning managers to find that their foreign experience and skills count for little and that they are not especially well rewarded for their international service. In all probability, their jobs upon return will not involve the use of skills acquired abroad.

Solving the Repatriation Problem

As a result of the growing worldwide competition for sales and profits, international business expertise is becoming more important, even to traditional domestic companies. Even those without a formal commitment to globalized management are, therefore, beginning to improve their repatriation policies so as to retain executives with international capabilities. Attention is also being paid to creating career paths to accommodate managers who wish to remain abroad.

Experienced international human resources executives suggest that companies adopt the following priorities to address their repatriation problems.

Priority One: Value International Performance

Executives interviewed for this study say that the most important initiative companies can take to reduce repatriation problems is to enhance the status of international assignments. At those companies in which working abroad lacks prestige, successful repatriation is an uphill battle at best. In contrast, if going abroad is seen as a "plum" assignment—one that *increases*, rather than *decreases*, an executive's visibility and stature within the corporation—repatriation often goes more smoothly. When expatriates are successfully reintegrated into the home operation—and the employer is seen as trying hard to make that happen—the prospect of working overseas becomes more attractive. It is, in effect, a "virtuous cycle," in which the higher status accorded international service leads to more effective repatriation and vice versa.

Other, more formal ways to improve the status of international assignments include increasing the salaries of managers working abroad, developing recognition systems to single out individuals for superior performance and creating specialized training programs that give foreign managers access to top corporate officials. Most of all, top management should ensure that overseas personnel are fully integrated into the company's career-planning system. Nothing increases status, and hence employee satisfaction, as much as career advancement.

Priority Two: Make a Real Effort

Most companies say they do their best to find jobs for returning expatriates. In cases where the executive fails to receive a job, management often blames it on the individual. "The simple fact of the matter is that most of the people who don't work out bring it on themselves," says Henri C. Debuisser, executive director of personnel, organization and corporate affairs at *Rank Xerox.*

But once executives have been selected and sent overseas, they rapidly appreciate as an asset. Thus, it is also true that when an expatriate is left out in the cold without a new assignment, the company itself must concede some degree of failure: Its large investment in the employee has been for naught. Worse, that person is probably going to put his talents and knowledge, developed at the company's expense, in the service of a competitor. In short, it is worth a company's while to "go the extra mile" to find employees appropriate jobs when they return.

Debuisser agrees that "as usual in life, there is probably a little bit of shared responsibility." As a result, Rank Xerox is "careful to make sure that reentry problems are kept well under control. A failure to do so would kill our expatriate program."

In an effort to avert repatriation problems, *Dow Chemical Japan* has tried to incorporate repatriation concerns in its initial executive-selection process. In choosing the executives sent to Japan, the company tries to select employees who will not only succeed there, but will also find a job waiting at home.

But no matter how qualified an expatriate may be, he is often at a logistical disadvantage when it comes to learning about new assignments. Therefore, it is critical that someone pick up the slack. Although the corporate human resources staff may be the obvious choice, it often has trouble selling the expatriate internally, in part because it knows little about the executive's progress overseas. To bridge the gap between headquarters and overseas and to help repatriated managers adjust, many companies have adopted mentor programs.

Priority Three: Provide a Mentor

Mentoring provides expatriates, on a one-to-one basis, with senior executives who monitor their progress and watch out for their interests while they are abroad. Mentors—sometimes known as sponsors—follow expatriates' career development and accomplishments overseas, keep them posted on official and unofficial changes and goings-on at headquarters and serve as troubleshooting liaisons between them and various headquarters departments. Roughly one third of MNCs surveyed by MS&B report using senior executives as mentors in these capacities.

■ *Rank Xerox* states that the key role of sponsors is "to be a link between the assignee and the core unit, to keep him or her informed of what is going on at home and to take care of their reentry job," explains Debuisser. The company actually gives each expatriate two mentors, the second serving as a backup "in case one disappears for some reason." Sponsors may have one, two or several assignees; senior executives tend to have more than their middle-level counterparts. To a degree, the company gives assignees some leeway in selecting a sponsor.

Sponsors look after their assignees and help arrange their jobs upon return. An assignee, in turn, can call the sponsor if any problems arise. "For example," says Debuisser, "someone might call because he hasn't received the salary increase he was told to expect, and he wants to know if this means anything or if it's just a bureaucratic delay." Debuisser believes the program has been effective. Usually if someone does not receive a job offer, "it's because he has `irritated' the system, and people in a position to hire him—most of whom are part of the sponsor network—don't want to," he says.

- *AT&T* has also implemented a mentor program. "Each person who goes overseas now has a sponsor back here in the US," says Nancy Burgas, manager of global learning systems. "The sponsor is responsible for keeping that person informed of what's going on in the business." The company stipulates that mentors be at least two salary grades above the assignee. That way, says Burgas, "it's someone who's going to be a stable influence, so that even though you've left the organizational loop, you still have somebody to contact."

- *IBM* uses a system of "career managers" to watch over junior expatriates. "Normally," says Don Laidlaw, IBM's director of executive resources and development, "it's an executive in the organization you left, who is senior enough to make sure opportunities are identified for you before your assignment is completed." When the time comes for repatriation, the career manager "has a responsibility to make sure that human resources and the organization find the most appropriate assignment for you," says Laidlaw.

  Typically, IBM's career managers each have only one expatriate to monitor, which enables them to fulfill their obligations and leaves them no excuse to neglect their charge. IBM makes it clear to mentors that this responsibility is an integral part of their jobs.

- *Colgate-Palmolive* adopted a pilot mentor program about three years ago, whose goal was, and remains, to promote closer relations between senior and junior managers. "The primary focus is the global marketing trainees, as well as new outside hires," says Whitaker. "It's not mandatory," Whitaker says. "We are mainly looking to support our international management cadre at the early stages of their careers. Once they are back at headquarters, they typically develop other, more informal, ties to people who are more powerful and enduring than the assigned relationships with mentors."

Other Mentoring Approaches. Other companies have opted for a more informal approach to mentoring. At *Atlas Copco,* you often find former boss-subordinate relationships that develop into mentor ones. These often last for many years, even if the two individuals no longer work together.

Although *Philips* does not have a formal mentor system, it makes line managers responsible for the personal development of expatriates that serve under them. Generally, it is the responsibility of the "home product division" or "home country" to define the next job prior to the expiration of their service abroad. In addition, however, the human resources department also keeps an eye on the progress of people working overseas and tries to place them in positions prior to the end of their overseas assignment.

In a similar vein, *Fuji Xerox* has established a special personnel section devoted to ensuring fulfillment of the education, housing and other needs of the 130 Japanese expatriates serving in the firm's offshore subsidiaries. As part of continuing efforts to "get feedback and see how they can help with problems," managers from this section try to visit every overseas location once every two years. Such visits allow managers to examine firsthand both the requirements of local personnel and the background of complaints. For example, explains Fuji Xerox's Haraguchi, "in the Philippines, it's common for expatriates to hire domestic help, whereas in Japan, such a practice would be almost unthinkable. So if an overseas assignee complains that he needs more money for domestic help, we are in a position to evaluate the claim."

Priority Four: Make a Formal Job Commitment

A step beyond mentor programs is the buy-back procedure. Under this method, companies pledge, often in writing, to give returning executives jobs of equivalent responsibility to those they held overseas, usually in the executives' former business unit. The chief advantage of a buy-back program is that it reduces employee doubt about whether to accept an international assignment. Moreover, the job guarantee frees the executive, while abroad, from worrying about the details of a looming repatriation.

The downside of a buyback is that it may breed inertia. People whose subsequent jobs are guaranteed may not search out positions on their own. Moreover, human resources personnel may be lulled into a sense of complacency about the development of overseas executives. Some observers contend guarantees produce stagnation and increased bureaucracy. To guard against this problem, companies often insist that the human resources department aggressively try to devise imaginative assignments and provide additional training to help returnees accomplish new job goals.

- *AT&T* has developed one of the largest buy-back programs. In light of the company's traditional domestic orientation, the program has helped make its growing overseas operations attractive to talented domestic employees. "It has become a common practice that when employees go out on international assignments, they take with them a buy-back letter from their home organization," says AT&T's Bibiana Santiago, human resources director for Europe. "The buy-back letter can vary, depending on the individual and circumstances. The guarantee is usually quite general, but it does include a statement to the effect that the company is willing to return the person to the same business unit at a specified date."

    Returning to their previous operations is considered only one of the employees' options, however. Once overseas, says Santiago, executives "often work closely with many different business sectors and business units that happen to be housed at a single location." Thus, they become familiar with AT&T businesses to which they might not have been exposed in the US. As a result, "by the time they go home, they may be willing or even eager to change business sectors. This contrasts with managers who spend their whole careers working in the same building for the same business unit."

    At the junior-executive level, repatriation is normally handled by the executive's own business unit. However, if there are problems with placement, it becomes a corporate issue.

- *Philips* is another convert to the buy-back approach. According to J. D. de Leeuw, the managing director of the corporate staff bureau, it works as follows: "If a young marketing manager from the lighting division is being expatriated, he gets a kind of return guarantee signed by a senior executive in the lighting division. So, in essence, his job is sponsored by the lighting division." The company does not guarantee a specific job, only the right to have a suitable position upon return. In the unlikely event that there is simply no job available in the sponsoring division, "we try to find him a job in another division," says de Leeuw. "If that doesn't work, then the final strategy is to find a temporary solution, such as a project."

Priority Five: Stay in Touch With Expatriates

Another way to ease repatriation is to prevent a communications gap from developing between expatriates and headquarters. A liberal home-leave policy, as well as ample opportunities to attend conferences, travel on business or interact frequently with headquarters people by phone and fax, can help the expatriate keep up with friends and colleagues. Through such contacts, managers who work overseas often learn about job opportunities at home and are able to line up appropriate return positions on their own.

- *Atlas Copco's* vice president of group staff personnel Nils-Åke Jenstav states that, "Atlas Copco sponsors conferences for all our management people, which focus on their specialties. Some functional fields, such as financial management, have international conferences almost every year." Conferences are designed to promote synergy by bringing managers from different countries and business units together in an informal atmosphere and by providing training to improve skills. "Whenever there is a new system or a particular achievement that we would like to share with them, we put on a conference," says Jenstav. A side benefit, of course, is that managers at foreign subsidiaries can mix and mingle with their counterparts from headquarters.

- *Acer* in Taiwan has also developed a wide variety of methods to keep expatriates in touch with developments at headquarters. Says John Wang, senior vice president for corporate administration: "We send them copies of *Acer News,* which is a biweekly on company products and strategy, and a cross-cultural monthly magazine, *Spectrum,* which focuses exclusively on cultural perceptions and practices in each country where we operate. We hope that over time, employees in each country in which we operate will provide input to this publication."

Home Leave. One of the most important ways to keep people in touch with headquarters is home leave. Most companies provide home leave once a year and generally allow expatriates to combine it with regular vacation. Home leave is usually accompanied by the scheduling of visits with senior executives at headquarters. Home leave and vacation lengths typically vary according to certain criteria—the person's position, the country where the person works or the person's home country. At *Rank Xerox,* for example, it depends on "the policy of the home country," says Debuisser. "So if you're an Austrian, you get six weeks of home leave, but if you're from the US, you get less."

Repatriation Planning and Assistance

According to the MS&B study, only 11% of MNCs surveyed provide formal repatriation training, although some 31% offer informal assistance in the form of a "buddy system." In the latter, an executive back at home is charged with helping a returning executive adjust, not unlike similar systems that pair old hands with newly arrived expatriates overseas. Although informal assistance is useful, companies that do provide formal repatriation training report that it has proven invaluable in easing the transition to a new work and home environment.

Ideally, repatriation planning should begin even before executives have left for overseas postings. By preparing executives in advance for the entire cycle of an international assignment, a company facilitates the successful completion of this vital last leg of the process.

■ *Rank Xerox.* Besides the difficulty of finding an appropriate job, perhaps the biggest problem executives encounter upon their return is a redefinition of their status. In some cases this is substantial. "When an executive goes abroad, especially to a Third World country, he sometimes gets delusions of grandeur," says Rank Xerox's Debuisser. "He is given special pay or allowances, he has a car and driver and household servants—perhaps a maid, a cook, a gardener, a nanny—and he becomes accustomed to being a VIP. But on the other hand, the cultural amenities he and his family are used to at home may not exist, and social relationships may be hard to develop. Psychologically, life can be tough.

"When the executive returns, he may experience both irritation, because the VIP perks are no longer there, and a feeling of entitlement, because of the difficulties endured abroad. He may think he's now entitled to `graze.' It is common to hear comments like: `Look at what I went through for this company.' Or, `I built that business. I was a general manager.' In many cases, readjustment is difficult.

"To avoid that, we sit each prospective expatriate down in advance and say, `Look, you're going to be a big shot when you go there, but you should be prepared for what you will face when you get back.'"

■ *Acer's* Wang agrees. For an expatriate, "the emperor is far away, so the expatriate is the `king' in his own domain," he observes. "But once he returns, he's a foot soldier again. Returnees often become dissatisfied with their life at home, because living standards and environmental conditions abroad may have been better than in Taiwan." Initially, the management of the fast-growing computer firm "didn't have time to cope with this," acknowledges Wang, "so a small number of people left. But now we do things better. We talk to returnees before they come home about what kind of job they will have back in Taiwan and what the potential for advancement and personal growth is."

Perhaps more important, Acer's corporate administration department can offer housing and educational assistance if requested by a returning employee. Moreover, the firm plans to establish a program of peer interchange that will, among other things, provide briefings for returning expatriates on Acer's strategic goals and how these fit into their new job responsibilities.

- *AT&T*, too, believes in the value of interchange among former expatriates. Returnees attend a repatriation seminar with their peers within six months of arriving back home. The seminar deals with adjustment to the home culture and allows returning expatriates to share their experiences with others who are faced with reassimilation into the large home organization.

    Because repatriation is merely a part of the entire cycle of an overseas assignment, AT&T is currently fashioning an integrated program of training for executives that will link predeparture training, training overseas, repatriation training and postrepatriation training in the form of a total training cycle. "The program looks at the whole cycle of an international assignment," explains AT&T's Brussels-based Santiago. "The in-country part of training will deal with assimilation, stress management, career planning and the working environment." During the course of an assignment, the "focus of the program changes," says Santiago. "The first year of an assignment is more of a counseling session than a training session. The program focuses more on...settling into the new environment. As executives go through their assignments and are closer to repatriation, the format changes to one of `You're about to go back.'" A new workshop has also been developed to prepare executives for the challenges of reentry.

- *GM's* repatriation planning also begins with predeparture training. In addition to discussing adjustment to life abroad, "we also talk about the reverse culture shock families frequently experience when readjusting to the US culture," says GM's Fisher.

    Some companies choose to contract out for help with repatriation of executives. MS&B is one of a number of consulting firms that offer programs for executives who have been recently repatriated.

The MS&B reentry program for repatriated executives and their families, used by a number of large MNCs, lasts two days and includes discussions of changes in executives' companies, the US, their families and themselves, which have occurred during their assignment overseas. Executives are encouraged to examine their attitude toward the company, their new assignment and their work situation and develop constructive plans for adjusting to and becoming more effective on the job.

■ *NEC*'s Institute of Management has implemented its own extensive "postrepatriation" program designed to "help returning executives adapt to the Japanese environment again as soon as possible," says Masaru Yamamoto, general manager for international education. The institute's course for returning overseas assignees focuses on "current issues and policies for each business group, presented by a speaker from each of the groups. In this way, the returnees can refresh their knowledge of industry developments and find out what happened in NEC and in their own departments while they were away from Japan."

Family Help: The Stress Is on Schooling

As noted earlier, children's education is a major issue for executives who are returning from an international assignment. Often, when children have received a pivotal portion of their schooling abroad, moving them back to conventional schools at home can be problematic. Most companies say that coping with this problem is expensive, and if handled through a blanket policy, could create troublesome precedents for "compensation" for any family member inconvenienced by an international move. For this reason, Rank Xerox addresses schooling problems on a case-by-case basis.

The problem of schooling is particularly acute for children of Japanese executives. Examinations to enter top-quality public secondary and tertiary schools in Japan are highly competitive and often prove difficult for children educated abroad. As a result, many Japanese executives go overseas alone and leave their families at home. Says Fuji Xerox's Haraguchi, "entry into junior high and senior high school poses the most serious problems. In Kanagawa prefecture, for example, if a student wants to get into a public high school, he or she must have scores from the second-year exams in junior high. You can't get into high school without those scores! But they don't have those tests in the US." To help resolve such problems, Xerox's

Rochester, New York office runs a Japanese school; elsewhere, the company tries to find schools for Japanese students and provides necessary financial assistance.

Another tack companies may take is to develop relationships with schools to facilitate readmittance. It is certainly crucial that companies at least keep their employees aware of these concerns so that parents can take action in advance. NEC offers a one-day program for families to address the issue of schools. In addition, it has also hired an educational consultant to speak with expatriate parents, while they are still abroad, about their children's education.

Educational difficulties are not limited to the Japanese, however. A case in point, the daughter of a US expatriate spent her teenage years in French-speaking countries and attended local schools, because her parents believed these schools provided a more rigorous education than the "international" schools located in those countries. As a result, she had to spend a year in the US after high school studying American history, which she had never learned, and English, which for her was a second language, in order to gain admission to a selective US college.

Alternative to Repatriation: Global Career Pathing

For many MNCs, an increasingly attractive alternative to repatriation is keeping executives abroad. Rather than force an internationally minded executive back into an unsuitable job at headquarters, it may be more advisable to rotate that person among overseas assignments.

In fact, long-term or multiple assignments abroad are not new. On the contrary, many companies have traditionally employed a cadre of long-term international executives. Such individuals often came from third countries rather than from the company's home country. Such individuals constituted a breed unto themselves as distinct from the regular one- or two-assignment expatriate. In the days before host governments began putting sustained pressure on MNCs to hire locally, some managers remained overseas indefinitely. Some even became permanent expatriates, establishing deep roots in the local community and becoming true experts in doing business in a particular country or region.

This was the practice at one large European MNC for many years. Until recently, the computer firm had permanent expatriates filling high positions, particularly in Latin America. In some cases, it designated certain positions, such as financial director or technical director, to be filled by long-term expatriates only. Today, however, the company is reducing its maximum term for an assignment to five years.

What is new today is that long-term executives are more likely to move around than stay in one place. With the onset of globalization strategies, foreign service is seen as a prime executive training ground. Expatriates now fill developmental positions overseas that may ultimately lead to a top position at headquarters. As the world grows smaller, once-sleepy outposts have become areas of important growth and, therefore, excellent places to cultivate executive talent. Thus, instead of languishing in some far-flung country, managers are increasingly sent from one country to another, with the enthusiastic support of the corporate human resources staff, as part of a planned career-development strategy.

A proponent of this new approach is *Coca-Cola*. "We always had a cadre of international executives," says director of human resources development D. Larry Kroh. However, these permanent expatriates are giving way to expatriates on the move, executives for whom an international assignment is just one stage in a career. Although many expatriates in the past were third-country nationals, today "US citizens who want the international experience are growing in numbers," he adds.

How Long Is Long Enough?

This new trend toward global career pathing has led to changes in the average length of foreign assignments. Today, they are rarely open ended. Most companies have established a fairly standard term for assignments, which ranges from two to six years. In its 1989 repatriation survey, MS&B reported that the average length of international assignments among the firms interviewed was three years. A fixed term reassures the expatriate, who otherwise might fear the commitment imposed by an indefinite assignment. It also helps to attract highly ambitious people to international service, as opposed to drawing only from the ranks of those who fancy themselves "internationalists" or country specialists or those who simply want to live abroad for a while. From the company's management-development perspective, a fixed term ensures that the executive will receive a prescribed amount of exposure to a particular market and then presumably graduate to another assignment elsewhere.

However, companies differ in the length of assignment they consider preferable. Indeed, the average length of assignments at companies surveyed by MS&B ranged from one year to six years. *Coca-Cola*'s D. Larry Kroh says that at his company most international postings last three to five years. "Obviously, the cost of moving somebody for anything less than that becomes pretty steep," he says.

At Taiwan's *Acer*, an overseas assignment lasts "usually two or three years for a sales and marketing management job," says Wang, although this period can be extended. Technical assignments, however, are typically shorter, averaging one year. *IBM* assignments on average last two to three years.

One advantage of the shortest assignments, those in the two-to-three-year range, is that they keep a tighter rein on distant employees and require less personal sacrifice from them. An important disadvantage, however, is that executives are unlikely to see the results of their work in only a couple of years. This is particularly true for subsidiary general managers and equivalent high-level jobs.

- *Rank Xerox* is a proponent of longer assignments at more senior levels. "The basic contract is two years minimum, with the general assumption that it will be three years," says Debuisser. "But a general manager should go for at least three to four years. We feel that a manager needs that length of time for several reasons: The first year he's working on somebody else's operating plan. The second year he's working on his own plan, but we don't want him to just do a plan for one year. We want him to build on that plan for longer-term results."

  Another important argument in favor of longer assignments is cost. "Let's not overlook the financial element," Debuisser says. "You must amortize the cost over as long a time as possible. So at six months, you'd have a horrendous cost, whereas three years is more reasonable."

- *Bull's* foreign assignments last three to five years. The company believes that a longer assignment is necessary to accomplish anything meaningful. "Two years is too short for succeeding as an expatriate, so assignments usually last three years," says a Bull senior manager.

- *Philips* also believes in longer assignments, typically four years. Although the company may send out executives for shorter periods, "these aren't really international assignments," de Leeuw says, "but just a specific task to be completed. If you're talking about a career assignment, it's typically four years, but often five or six at senior levels. In a career assignment, a person should have the opportunity to show accomplishment, and that's not possible in two or three years."

- *NEC* also observes the same standard. Typical overseas postings run for "four to six years on average, though there are people who stay much longer," says Hajime Hasegawa, senior vice president and director of the NEC Institute of Management.

- *AT&T* sends people out on assignments for differing lengths of time, depending on the job's requirements. "The goal of AT&T is to minimize the number of expatriates throughout the world," says Santiago. As a result, the firm's expatriates are likely to have either managerial or technical ability. When managerial assignees "go over on assignment," says Santiago, "it's typically because we're starting up an activity or they need to teach the AT&T system and philosophy." Such assignments tend to be of longer duration, usually three to five years. On the other hand, technical assignments tend to be at a lower level and cover a specific need. As a result, they typically last only two to three years.

  AT&T also has a plan to enable expatriates to become, in effect, local employees. "Overseas assignees can become declassified as expatriates. It's the employee's decision if he or she wants to stay in a particular country outside of his or her home," says Santiago. "If so, the firm can phase them out of expatriate status and onto a local plan," though, as a rule, the firm prefers local hires for posts of indefinite duration. "If the company wants to keep an employee on away from home, that's a different story, and they would stay on expatriate status," she adds.

- *Dow Chemical's* average assignment length for staffers can vary, depending in part on location. "For example," says Peter J. Cohen, director of human resources and administrative services for Dow Chemical Japan, "executives here typically stay somewhat longer than those posted elsewhere." Dow's practice of using indefinite assignments instead of contracts covering a fixed period of time is unusual among MNCs. Says Cohen, "An assignment expected to last three to four years may thus stretch into quite a long time." Cohen believes there may be some advantages to a fixed-term system, because it could help "resolve, or at least clarify, the repatriation issue to some extent."

Number of Assignments Abroad

Despite companies' growing recognition that the best way to use seasoned international executives is to give them new foreign assignments, there is also widespread acknowledgment that too much time spent overseas may result in an employee's "going native"; or the expatriate may simply fall out of touch with strategy shifts at the parent company.

- *Atlas Copco*'s management generally likes to limit a person to two overseas assignments in a row. For example, "when it comes to financial managers," says Jenstav, "we try to make it a pattern that after two assignments, totaling, say, six to eight years, they go back to group headquarters for one or two more years to meet the new executives who have joined the company in the interim, look into new systems and so forth." The reason is simply that "if you are in a remote country too long, you're uninformed about what's going on at corporate headquarters and, even more, in the business groups," Jenstav says. He points out that although managers may be conducting their business in a satisfactory manner, they are often too distant from what their counterparts at home are thinking about. In addition, expatriates may require training in new methods or systems, which sometimes can be difficult to administer abroad.

However, as some companies decentralize their operations in the context of a global strategy, the notion of "headquarters" may only mean a regional office. Thus, at Atlas Copco, an executive interested in advancing in the compressor business would look to Belgium headquarters for compressors.

Japan: Test Case for Career Pathing

Japanese companies are facing up to the challenge of bringing non-Japanese executives into headquarters. There are many obstacles to full integration of non-Japanese personnel into Japanese companies, besides the more obvious linguistic and cultural differences. In particular, corporate recruitment systems, implicit lifetime employment compacts and rigid seniority systems that still characterize most major Japanese firms require a commitment on the part of employees that by North American or European standards is unusual. Nobuo Umeoka, assistant general manager of MEI's corporate personnel department, says, "The biggest area that we have to improve on is the career-path program. We Japanese who are working in Japan can see the career path for ourselves. But the American students we hope to attract in the US still cannot see what their career path after joining the company will be."

However, Umeoka notes that personnel practices are changing in many Japanese companies. "In the past, major Japanese companies followed seniority rules and the lifetime employment system very rigidly, but today serious cracks in these systems are emerging." He adds, "In the future, the employment structure in Japan will probably become closer to that of Europe and the US."

Creating the Global Executive

MNCs are moving away from stagnant, long-term overseas postings and toward global career paths that involve successive, increasingly responsible positions abroad. The objective is to help high-potential managers hone their skills and build knowledge that may one day be useful in a top job at a major subsidiary or at corporate headquarters.

This trend accords well with the ideal of globalization being pursued by many MNCs. No longer can distant markets be written off as backwaters. They must be served and developed by the best talent a company has; in turn, they provide managers with important and varied on-the-job training.

Philips typifies the global company that not only appreciates international expertise, but also demands it. "Increasingly, we make it clear that anyone who wants a senior position in this company has to gain experience in foreign locations," says de Leeuw. "We tell our people that if they don't want a job in a foreign country, that will have consequences for their careers. The higher one climbs at Philips, the more global one has to think and the more international one's experience has to be."

At *Colgate-Palmolive,* a majority of the top executives have extensive global experience. For example, CEO Reuben Mark was once general manager in Venezuela and later vice president for Europe; COO William S. Shanahan was formerly general manager in Brazil; and CFO Robert M. Agate, a British citizen, has worked in Malaysia, India, Australia and various European countries. Says Whitaker, "Not everyone has to be a global manager, but certainly those who are setting strategy need to be. We are not casual about this global issue."

Hajime Hasegawa of the *NEC* Institute of Management insists that "international service is not a detour, but a shortcut. Overseas assignments form an important and honorable part of a career path in NEC." Masahiro Haraguchi of Fuji Xerox also believes that a posting abroad may prove to be a shortcut for young executives, but "for an older executive, it could be a detour."

With the growing emphasis on youth and globalization, there can be little doubt that international experience will become more and more coveted in coming years. MNCs who wish to emerge as key leaders in the global economy of tomorrow would do well to heed this trend.

Advanced Management Programs and Executive Education Courses Offered at Universities

A Selection

Ashridge Management College
Berkhamsted, Hertfordshire
UK HP4 1NS
Tel: (4444) 284-3491
Fax: (4444) 284-2382

Management-Development Program (four weeks)

Action Learning for Chief Executives and Directors (six days)

European Management Program (two weeks)

Directors' Program (five days)

International Managers' Program (two weeks)

Strategic Management Program (three weeks)

Strategic Decisions (five days)

Group Level Strategy (five days)

Columbia University Graduate School of Business
Columbia Executive Programs
Columbia University
324 Uris Hall
New York, NY 10027
Tel: (212) 854-3395
Fax: (212) 316-1473

Senior-Level General
Management Programs

Executive Program in Business Administration (EPBA): Managing the Enterprise, four weeks, offered twice annually

Executive Program in International Management (EPIM): Managing for Global Success, four weeks, offered once annually

Business Strategy

Business Strategy, two weeks, offered once annually

International Strategy: Winning Globally, one week, offered twice annually

Achieving the Sustainable Turnaround, one week, offered once annually

Leadership and Change

Managing Strategic Innovation and Change, one week, offered twice annually

Leading and Managing People, one week, offered twice annually

Creating the Customer-Oriented Firm, one week, offered once annually

Managing Cultural Diversity, one week, offered once annually

Managing Business Processes: Improving Product and Service Quality, one week, offered once annually

Functional Management

Marketing Management, one week, offered six times annually

Sales Management, one week, offered three times annually

Marketing Analysis for Competitive Advantage, one week, offered once annually

Managing Operations for Competitive Advantage, one week, offered once annually

Accounting and Financial Management for the Non-Financial Executive, one week, offered three times annually

Financial Management, one week, offered once annually

Human Resource Management: Effecting Change Beyond the 1990s, one week, offered once annually

European Programs (programs offered in conjunction with CIS Centro Studio D'Impresa at Lake Como, Italy)

Marketing Management, one week, offered once annually

Managing Strategic Innovation and Change, one week, offered once annually

Managing Turnarounds and Strategic Alliances, one week, offered once annually

International Strategy, one week, offered twice annually

Financial Policy in the Global Market, one week, offered once annually

Sample Courses

Executive Program in International Management (EPIM): Managing for Global Success. This intensive, four-week program with top-level participants and faculty is presented within a unified conceptual framework for maximum efficiency.

The world's longest-running program for international executives, the program is designed to help executives succeed in the global marketplace. Skills are developed in four major areas: formulating strategy, managing the functional areas, managing people and managing in the international environment. The organization of the program is intended to weave these skills together for effective application.

Participants in the program are senior general managers, country managers or functional managers who wish to broaden their busi-ness viewpoints. Typically, organizations represented are located throughout the world and offer products or services to both industrial and consumer markets. The diversity in backgrounds is designed to enrich the formal and informal discussions held throughout the program.

Columbia cites the following as benefits of attending. Participants are taught:

How to identify, develop and defend an international competitive advantage

The major forces leading to globalization of industries

Implications of changes in the European community

How to use financial analysis as a competitive tool

How social, demographic and political trends will impact their global strategy

How specific companies have succeeded internationally

The key questions for understanding international customers

How to develop effective business strategies for country, regional and global markets

How, where and when to enter markets

What the crucial considerations are regarding the integration of financing and marketing strategies

How to understand cultural differences and their implications for strategy

In addition, many other subjects are stressed including how to deal with stress and economic and political events as well as how to manage joint ventures.

Ideas are conveyed through discussion and exercises. Experts provide leading-edge concepts and viewpoints while applications exercises are used to help participants develop strategies for their own businesses. In addition, participants form teams to develop action plans and strategies to cope with simulated business situations. The course covers the following four themes and sub-themes:

- Assessing the global environment

  Appraising global, economic, cultural, political, social, demographic and technological changes

  Evaluating global customers and competitors, now and into the future

  Identifying forces transforming industries to global or multi-domestic status

- Managing the functional areas

  Applying state-of-the-art tools of financial analysis

  Designing powerful marketing strategies through targeting and through informed application of programs such as pricing, sales force and advertising

  Setting operations policy to achieve high productivity

- Managing people

  Organizing, managing and motivating people so that they will perform at a high level in complex international environments

  Understanding the key factors that lead to high performance

  Implementation: transforming strategy into action

  Facilitating cross-cultural interaction and teamwork

  Managing oneself to achieve company and personal goals

- Developing global strategy

  Formulating international business strategies that are successful in achieving objectives over time

  Coping with risks that are specifically international, such as politics, culture or exchange rates

  Orchestrating international product service, pricing and communications strategies

  Designing and managing international organizations that are flexible and dynamic

  Managing Cultural Diversity. This one-week course is designed to provide managers with insights into the cultural differences that people bring to the workplace as well as to help managers understand and incorporate others' views to promote teamwork and maximize productivity. The course is predicated on the notion that managing a diverse workforce and gaining market share in a global economy requires high-functioning intercultural teams. As a result, participants explore the intellectual, emotional and behavioral dimensions of managing culturally diverse teams. Managerial skills are assessed by examining how we experience individual ethnic, gender, national and international differences; how we communicate our attitudes and beliefs; and how we resolve intercultural programs.

Participants include senior- and mid-level executives who must develop teams in a workplace—domestic or international—characterized by increasing cultural diversity.

Methods used in the course include lecture group discussion, case study, self-reporting, individual coaching and small-group exercises. Some work sessions are videotaped and analyzed for the purpose of exploring the dynamics of different world views and how they affect team productivity. These methods are designed to develop conceptual tools to understand intercultural problems. The format also includes a team-consultation model that helps participants examine organizational issues and develop action plans.

Columbia cites the following as benefits of attending. The course is designed to provide managers with:

A practical understanding of the meaning that work and achievement have for different groups

A framework for diagnosing organizational issues about cultural diversity

Knowledge and tools for innovating and maintaining a process for more effective teamwork

The course covers the following themes and sub-themes:

- Developing Intercultural Managerial Skills
- Differences in World View and Team Functioning

   Assessment of each participant's world view using an instrument called SAWV (Ibrahim & Kahn, 1984)
   Comparison of white female and male sex role orientations
   Plans for improving gender relationships on the job
   Implications of world-view conflicts

■ Managing Diversity and Overcoming Barriers to Change

Harvard Business School
Executive Education Programs
Harvard University
Soldiers Field - Glass Hall
Boston, MA 02163
Tel: (617) 495-6226
Fax: (617) 495-6999

Comprehensive General Management Programs

The Advanced Management Program, eleven weeks, offered twice annually

The International Senior Management Program (ISMP), nine weeks, offered once annually

The Program for Management Development (PMD), twelve weeks, offered twice annually

The Owner/President Management Program (OPM), three weeks, offered once annually

Workshops for General Managers

Performance Improvement Workshops

Managing Business Transformation, one week, offered once annually

Achieving Breakthrough Service (ABS), nine days, offered once annually

Building Development Capabilities (BDC), one week, offered once annually

Managing Global Opportunities: Mexico, three weeks, offered once annually

Executive Program in Competition and Strategy (CS), one week, offered once annually

Leadership Workshops

Agribusiness Seminar, four days, offered once annually

How to Get More Out of Your Board, four days, offered once annually

Seminar for Top Management in Retailing, four days, offered once annually

Advanced Functional Courses

Strategic Cost Management (SCM), one week, offered once annually

Strategic Marketing Management (SMM), two weeks, offered once annually

Corporate Financial Management (CFM), two weeks, offered once annually

Strategic Human Resource Management (HRM), one week, offered twice annually

Manufacturing in Corporate Strategy (MCS), two weeks, offered once annually

Managing the Information Services Resource (MISR), two weeks, offered once annually

Sample Courses

Advanced Management Program. This intensive, eleven-week program is designed to prepare senior executives for the challenges of corporate leadership. The program is designed to provide participants with the tools, knowledge and insights needed to lead corporate enterprises in an era of rapid corporate transition and increasing global competition.

The program reflects three basic premises about the work of top-level managers. The first is that the tasks of defining, creating and distributing value for the constituencies comprising the enterprise are primary responsibilities of general management. In this regard, the AMP explores innovative policy and administrative practices in different settings in order to help managers usefully define and create value and otherwise enhance corporate performance.

The second premise is that general management tasks cannot be accomplished without understanding how the ever-changing political, economic, social and cultural environment affects choices and operations. For this reason, the AMP examines the institutions and policies through which governments endow business with authority and control its activities.

The third premise is that the modern corporation acts in a complex moral setting. The AMP pays careful attention to the ethical aspects of business behavior. Individual executives' activities are depicted in case studies, allowing participants to examine their own beliefs and values.

The program targets executives from companies with annual revenues of $100 million or more. Most have 15 to 25 years of management experience. About one half are from North America while the remainder come from around the world. Participants are usually high-ranking corporate officers with titles such as executive vice president, senior vice president or group vice president, top functional officers with titles such as senior vice president, vice president or director or managers of major business units with titles such as general manager or division president.

The primary learning method used is the case method. Each case describes an actual management situation on which a decision must be made. Through careful analysis and discussion, participants formulate strategies to deal with them. Cases are based on field research in business organizations and the companies represented come from the manufacturing and service sectors. Cases are updated each year. Participants study the cases through informal discussions, formal discussion groups and classroom analysis before peers.

Topics covered include the following:

- Competition and strategy
- Business, government and the international economy
- Leadership and human resources
- Corporate financial management
- Marketing management
- Information, organization and control systems
- Technology and operations strategy

Managing Global Opportunities: Mexico and the North American Free Trade Area, 1993. This three-week course, which changes its focus annually, is designed to teach participants how to react to important international developments. In 1993, it will examine the implications of the North American Free Trade Agreement for corporate managers.

Admission to the program is highly selective. The program targets individual executives or teams responsible for managing foreign subsidiaries and/or managing product lines or operations that cross international boundaries. Professional position, achievement, promise and the overall need for balancing class composition are the main criteria for admission. Participants must be sponsored by a company and English-language proficiency is required.

Teaching methods include lectures and discussions as well as visits to Mexican companies and factories in order to learn how their ideas may apply in practice. The first two weeks of the program take place at the Harvard Business School campus in Cambridge. Teaching methods here include lectures and discussions. Topics covered include:

- Global strategy
- Global economy
- Multinational organization
- International finance
- International manufacturing
- International marketing

In addition, participants explore such issues as building global brands with local customization, the impact of cultural sensitivities on cross-border business, the dynamics of emerging trading blocks, dealing in an internationalized capital market and NAFTA's impact on US manufacturers.

After two weeks in Cambridge, the program moves to Mexico. In Guadalajara, participants spend three days gaining hands-on experience with visits to companies and factories in order to learn how their ideas may apply in practice. In turn, the program moves to Mexico City where course participants and faculty combine teaching with meetings with government and business leaders.

IMD-International Institute for Management Development
Chemin de Bellerive 23
PO Box 915 CH-1001
Lausanne, Switzerland
Tel: (4121) 618 0111
Fax: (4121) 618 0707

IMD divides its course offerings into the four categories listed below. Its MBA program for experienced managers is included under the category, Managing the Corporation while its Partnership Programs consisting of customized programs for given companies or groups of companies are included under the category, Implementing Change. The latter are described in detail below. All IMD courses are given in English.

Managing the Corporation

International Program for Board Members (IPBM), three days, offered twice a year

International Program for Senior Executives (IPSE), one week, offered three times a year

Job of the Chief Executive (JOCE), one week (held in Singapore), offered once a year

Seminar for Senior Executives (SSE), three weeks, offered twice annually

Managing Corporate Resources (MCR), four weeks, offered twice annually

Program for Executive Development (PED), two five-week modules, each module offered twice annually

Master of Business Administration (MBA), twelve months, offered every year

MBA Recruitment and International Consulting Projects (projects placing MBA graduates as consultants at corporations; available to graduates of the MBA program only), varying length, offered throughout the year

Developing Managerial Competence

Managing Competitive Strategy (MCS), one week, offered twice annually

Mobilizing People (MP), two weeks, offered twice annually

Leading the Family Business (LFB), three and one-half days, offered twice annually

Workshop on Business Alliances (WBA), three days, offered once annually

Implementing Change

International Executive Program (IEP), three weeks, offered twice annually

Partnership Programs, varying lengths, offered throughout the year (see below)

Broadening Functional Expertise

Managing Human Resources (MHR), one week, offered once annually

Managing Finance and Control (MFC), two weeks, offered twice annually

Managing Marketing (MM), three weeks, offered twice annually

Managing Industrial Market Strategy (MIMS), two weeks, offered once annually

Managing Services (MS), two weeks, offered once annually

Managing the Sales Force (MSF), one week, offered twice annually

Managing Manufacturing (MMG), two weeks, offered twice annually

Managing Research and Development (MR&D), two weeks, offered twice annually

Partnership Programs (customized programs designed for specific companies or consortia)

In addition to its normal offerings, IMD offers a number of single-company and consortia programs developed to meet the needs of specific companies. IMD gives priority in establishing such programs to its Sponsor and Business Associate companies.

The length of partnership programs can vary. Typical topics include general management, strategy formulation, marketing, finance, human resources and technology management. The participants group for a single-company program typically contains senior executives from headquarters as well as operating units and divisions. IMD typically charges a one-time development fee plus a fixed amount per week of the program. Most companies contract for a minimum of three offerings spread over a year or longer.

In addition to single-company programs, IMD also offers consortium programs attended by participants from more than one company. Typically, five or six companies, each sending up to ten participants, are recruited by IMD with the collaboration of the founding companies. Most consortia consist of non-competing companies. Two types of consortium programs are currently offered by IMD. They are its Joint Development programs, two-week, general management programs held at IMD, and its Consortium Program for Global Executives (CONGLOBE), a multi-location program whereby participants spend one week each in Eastern Europe, in the US, in Japan and at IMD.

Sample Courses

Managing Human Resources. This one-week course is designed to promote new thinking about HR practices and is focused on changes taking place in HR management. In particular, it examines general management's expectations of the function and how HR professionals can maximize their contributions. Topics addressed include new values and motivations in the work force, working effectively in teams, new business issues as they affect people and organizations, new forms of organization and career management in flatter organizations.

The program is designed to help HR managers do the following:

View the function from the perspective of general management

Understand how they can best contribute to the company

Appreciate the growing demand from younger people for rewarding employment and involvement

Develop new ways of thinking about the management of people and organizations

Recognize new values and orientations of individuals

Compare new forms of organization for the 1990s

Look at their contribution to new strategies

Participants are typically senior managers in the HR function and other senior executives who make policy decisions that directly affect human resources. Job titles of senior HR managers who take the program typically include Vice President of Personnel, Director of Organization Development, Director of Human Resource Strategy and Planning and Director of Management Development. Line managers with responsibility for the HR function will also benefit from the program. IMD stresses that the program is not designed to teach leadership skills or serve as an introduction to the HR function.

Learning methods include study groups and participatory learning techniques involving analysis of actual business situations. IMD believes that the wide distribution of nationalities and backgrounds of participants also serves to enhance the value of discussions.

Topics covered include:

- New paradigms of thought and organization
- New quality-based, time-based and customer-focused strategies
- New cultures
- New structures
- Managing careers in the new structure
- The HRM implications of business partnerships
- New styles of HRM in practice in Europe
- New competitive contexts
- Strategic human resource management

International Executive Program: Implementing Change in the Enterprise. This three-week course focuses on the opportunities and threats that face a company when it embarks on a program of fundamental change. It is intended for those who are about to lead a fundamental change process or who can benefit from a review of change underway. A primary benefit of the program is that it enables participants from different companies and levels of responsibility to discuss issues more openly and provocatively than is normally possible within a company. The executives look at the need for change, resistance to it, the management of change and the possibility of undertaking it to achieve competitive advantage.

The program is designed to help participants do the following:

Examine the need for change and the external factors that are driving it

Understand the various kinds of resistance at corporate and individual levels

Determine what kind of change process is most appropriate

Adopt a suitable strategy, change organization and implementation style

Trigger the action that makes change happen

Use the change process to diagnose and resolve problems

Set up the organizational capabilities that allow a company to lead change in the industry rather than merely react to it

Participants typically include executives who are or will soon be involved in managing substantial change within their companies. Age typically ranges from the mid-thirties to the early fifties and job titles and functions vary dramatically since change can affect any level of an organization. Companies may send teams of up to three people to the program.

Typical positions held by senior participants include: Managing director, senior director and general manager, director of administration and finance, vice president—business development, director of personnel. Typical positions held by junior participants include area manager—Middle and Near East, assistant general manager, assistant vice president—technology division, business manager, financial manager and sales manager.

Topics covered include the following:

- Week 1: Anticipating Change
  Forces of Resistance
  Drivers of Change
  Building Scenarios

- Week 2: Exploiting Change
  Different Intervention Paths
  Change Action Plans

- Week 3: Creating Change
  Proactive Realignment
  Developing Strategic Options
  Organizational Learning

Insead-Institute Europeen d'Administration des Affaires
Boulevard de Constance
F-77305 Fontainebleau
Cedex, France
Tel: (3316) 724273, (3316) 724290
Fax: (3316) 724242

Top Management Programs

AVIRA, five days, offered three times annually

Managing Multinational Enterprise (MME), three days, offered once annually

Leadership in Organizations (LIO), six days, offered three times annually

General Management Programs

Advanced Management Program (AMP), four weeks, offered four times annually

Advanced Management Program for Central Europe, one month, offered once annually

Advanced Management Program for Brazilian Executives, one week, offered four times annually

Alpha (a consortium program; one three-week and one two-week module), each module offered twice annually

International Executive Program (IEP), two weeks, offered twice or three times annually

Young Managers Program (YMP), three weeks, offered three or four times annually

Specialized Programs

Finance

International Corporate Finance (ICF), two weeks, offered once annually

Finance for Executives (FFE), two weeks, offered twice annually

Strategic Management in Banking (SMB), two weeks, offered once annually

Risk Management in Banking (RMB), one week, offered once annually

The Options Workshop, one week, offered three times annually

Human Resources and Organization

Managerial Skills for International Business (MSIB), two weeks, offered twice annually

Management of People (MOP), ten days, offered once annually

Marketing

European Marketing Program (EMP), three weeks, offered three times annually

Advanced Industrial Marketing Strategy (AIMS), two weeks, offered twice annually

Storwars: Strategies for Consumer Goods (Storwars), one week, offered twice annually

Marketing Management Seminar (MMS), two weeks, offered twice annually

Strategy

Strategic Issues in Mergers and Acquisitions (SIMA), one week, offered three times annually

Managing Partnerships and Strategic Alliances (MPSA), one week, offered three times annually

Strategic Cost Management (SCM), one week, offered once annually

Negotiation Dynamics (ND), one week, offered twice annually

Global Information and Telecommunications Industry: a strategic approach (GiTi), two weeks, offered once annually

Technology Management

International Manufacturing Program, three days, offered once annually

Strategic R&D Management (SRDM), two weeks, offered once annually

Other Programs

Company—Specific Programs

Euro-Asia Centre Programs

Management Strategy for a Sustainable Environment, three days, offered twice annually

Sample Courses

Advanced Management Program. This four-week program conducted in either English or French is designed to help senior executives achieve outstanding performance. The focus is on leveraging managerial and leadership skills, building confidence in managing strategic change and sharing knowledge on best international practices.

The program is targeted towards general managers who possess fifteen or more years' experience and, in most cases, an international career, as well as senior functional managers closely involved in the company's strategic decisions who have a broad business background. Participants typically have a profit and loss responsibility of over $50 million or head a function in a $150 million or more business and are part of a core management team. Typical job titles are managing director, general manager, head of technology, vice president strategy & planning, financial director, business unit manager, manager operations, sales and marketing manager, corporate vice president and corporate director human resources.

Topics covered include:

- Strategic management
- Financial management
- The economic environment of business
- Organizational behavior
- Marketing
- Operations management
- Strategic cost management
- Business in a political context

Specific issues include:

Deregulation and restructuring

The impact of 1992

Mergers, acquisitions and strategic alliances

Eastern Europe: what next?

Cross-cultural management

Insead believes that among the many advanced management programs offered worldwide, this is one of the few that offers a genuinely international perspective.

Young Managers Program. This three-week program conducted in either English or French is designed to provide high-potential young managers who already possess a good level of expertise in their own area with the knowledge and skills they will need to exercise higher managerial responsibilities successfully.

The program is targeted toward managers not more than 35 years old possessing an exceptional track record and, typically, at least five years' work experience. They should already enjoy considerable responsibility within their company. Typical job titles include: division manager, senior engineer, export sales manager, financial manager, product manager, marketing manager and technical director.

Initially the program concentrates on developing functional skills but emphasis is later placed on integrating these disciplines into general management concepts. Topics are discussed within an international frame of reference. Participants are exposed to problems outside their own specialized field through contact with faculty members and other managers representing a wide range of nationalities, cultures and educational backgrounds.

Topics covered include:

- Organizational behavior
- Marketing
- Finance and control
- Operations management
- Strategy and environment

Irish Management Institute
Sandyford Road
Dublin 16, Ireland
Tel: (3531) 956911
Fax: (3531) 955147 or 955150

Executive Development Program (five modules, each for five days over a period of five months)

J.L. Kellogg Graduate School of Management
Northwestern University
James L. Allen Center
Evanston, IL 60208-2800
Tel: (708) 491-3308

Executive Programs

Advanced Executive Program (four weeks)

International Advanced Executive Program (two weeks)

Executive Development Program (three weeks)

Executive Seminars (one week): topics include quality, communicating with the Japanese business world and many others

General Management

Advanced Executive Program, four weeks, offered twice annually

Executive Development Program, three weeks, offered three times annually

Managing the Closely Held Company in Changing Times: The Owner-Manager's Program, two weeks, offered once annually

Finance and Accounting

Corporate Financial Strategy, one week, offered once annually

Credit Analysis and Financial Reporting, six days in two parts, offered twice annually

Developing a Corporate Pension Strategy, one week, offered once annually

Managing Cost Information for Effective Strategic Decisions, four days, offered twice annually

Merger Week, one week, offered twice annually

Strategic Financial Planning, two days, offered once annually

Manufacturing and Technology

Developing Manufacturing's Strategic Potential, one week, offered once annually

Making Technology Work for the Organization, one week, offered once annually

Marketing

Business-to-Business Marketing Strategy, one week, offered twice annually

Communications Strategy: Managing Communications for the Changing Marketplace, one week, offered twice annually

Consumer Marketing Strategy, one week, offered twice annually

Increasing Sales Force Productivity, one week, offered twice annually

International Marketing Strategies, one week, offered twice annually

Negotiation and Dispute Resolution

Dispute Resolution for Attorneys, three days, offered once annually

Negotiation Strategies for Managers, four days, offered three times annually

Quality and Service

Creating World-Class Quality, one week, offered twice annually

Delivering Excellent Customer Service, one week, offered twice annually

Other Significant Programs

The Art of Venturing: Entrepreneurship in Corporate and Independent Settings, three days, offered three times annually

Communicating with the Japanese Business World, three days, offered twice annually

Decision-Making Strategies for Managers, four days, offered once annually

Company-Specific Programs

The Kellogg School is a leader in designing and conducting customized executive development programs for individual companies, industries and professional associations. Programs are typically designed and taught by a team of Kellogg School faculty with assistance from in-company personnel and other practitioners. They may range in length from one to four weeks and may be modular in format.

In addition to its menu of executive courses, The Kellogg School also offers The Executive Master's Program (EMP), a two-year general management program leading to the degree of Master of Management. It is designed for both midcareer executives reaching for senior management and senior managers. A class schedule of alternating Fridays and Saturdays allows participants to continue their careers while they study a broad range of management skills. The EMP admits two classes a year, one in September and one in January. It is taught by senior faculty members of the Kellogg School.

Sample Courses

International Marketing Strategies. This one-week program is designed to help companies develop managers who will become part of the powerful team of internationally knowledgeable and sophisticated managers required to succeed in the 1990s. It will provide these managers with an understanding of the marketing issues and approaches associated with the motto "think globally and act locally" in markets exhibiting very different cultural, political, economic and competitive characteristics.

The program has been designed to help participants meet the following objectives:

Develop an understanding of background and situational factors influencing international marketing effectiveness

Create and implement effective marketing strategies in response to the international environment

Monitor ongoing international marketing success and adapt international marketing programs where necessary

The program has been designed for managers who have been or will be given international marketing responsibilities or who can benefit from a more thorough understanding of international marketing. This includes international managers who have managed other functions such as finance, R&D and manufacturing, as well as domestic marketing managers who are assuming new international responsibilities. Participants come from a variety of industries and have different levels of marketing experience.

Interactive learning principles are stressed and participants are taught using discussions, cases, exercises, projects and group presentations. Participants meet in evening study groups with faculty assistance to prepare exercises and projects for class discussion.

Topics covered by the course include the following:

- Foreign market analysis of potential market size and profitability, competitive activity and country risk
- Identification of cultural, economic, political and legal challenges that distinguish international markets from each other and from the home market
- Analysis of available markets and modes of entry and their relative strengths and weaknesses
- Distribution channel design and choice of distribution partners

- Product design and adaptation for international markets, trading off market-by-market customization and global standardization

- Pricing strategies in different countries and regions including those to control gray market activity and the use of barter and counter-trade to clinch big-ticket sales

- Advertising and promotion planning for foreign markets

- Appropriate organizational structures and communications for international marketing

Communicating with the Japanese Business World. This two-day program runs from 3:45 PM on Sunday to noon on Tuesday and is designed to convey to participants detailed information about Japanese culture that they may use immediately in their business dealings.

It is designed for senior managers of corporations, professionals and government officials who are or will be dealing with the Japanese in the United States or Japan.

Program topics include the following themes and sub-themes:

- United States-Japan cross-cultural communications
- Various "types" of Japanese

First contact
Respective implications of phone/letter/face-to-face contact in Japan
Significance of using shokainin (introducer)
Japanese sense of what is a business meeting and what is a non-business meeting
What to do and what to avoid when the client first arrives at your company

- Meishi (business card) and related protocol
- Use of name suffixes
- How to use an interpreter
- Nonverbal language

Shaking hands or bowing
Typical Japanese gestures and their significance
Japanese use of silence

- How to give and receive compliments

- "Yes" and "no" in Japanese; ways to avoid saying "no" in Japanese
- Japanese etiquette

  Seating arrangements
  Table manners
  Unspoken dress code
  Giving and receiving goods

- Japanese psychology, patterns of thought and philosophy of certain behaviors
- Why Japanese appear ambivalent or indecisive
- Causes for Japanese loss of "face"
- Private truth and public facade
- Japanese sense of duty and obligation and of being considerate to others
- How Japanese hide their emotions
- Japanese male chauvinism, racism and aging
- Japanese sense of time and timing

  Apparent slowness in negotiations
  What to expect in the first meeting
  Announcing when to leave

- Japanese vertical versus American horizontal organizational structure

  Supremacy of personal relationship over individual competence
  Why joint ventures fail in Japan

- Japanese style of decision making: the importance of consensus seeking
- Japanese style of leadership
- Corporate rank system in Japan

The University of Michigan
The Michigan Business School
Executive Education Center
Ann Arbor, MI 48109-1234
Tel: (313) 763-1003
Fax: (313) 763-9467

Executive Development Programs

The Executive Program, four weeks

Public Utilities Executive Program, four weeks

Functional Executive Programs and Management Seminars

Accounting and Finance

Corporate Financial Management, one week, offered once annually

Activity-Based Costing for Improved Management Decision Making, one week, offered three times annually

Finance for the Non-Financial Manager, one week, offered four times annually

Financial Analysis, Planning and Control, one week, offered twice annually

Corporate Strategy

The Strategic Management of Technology, three days, offered twice annually

Strategy Formulation and Implementation, one week, offered twice annually

Operations Management

The Manufacturing Executive Program, two weeks, offered twice annually

Project Management, four days, offered three times annually

Strategic Quality Management Program, one week, offered twice annually

General Management

Program for Management Development: Managing Critical Issues, two weeks, offered twice annually

Creating Change: The Process of Corporate Revitalization, three days, offered four times annually

Executive Communication: Improving Speaking and Writing Skills, one week, offered twice annually

Basic Management for Newly Appointed Managers, three days, offered twelve times annually

Management II: A Mid-Management Development Program, one week, offered twelve times annually

Management of Managers, one week, offered twelve times annually

Effective Managerial Coaching and Counseling, three days, offered three times annually

Human Resources

Advanced Human Resources Executive Program, two weeks, offered once annually

Human Resource Executive Program, two weeks, offered twice annually

Strategic Human Resource Planning, one week, offered four times annually

Organizational Career Development, one week, offered three times annually

Interviewing: A Strategic Approach, three days, offered four times annually

The Instructional Development Workshop, one week, offered three times annually

Basic Wage and Salary Administration, three days, offered four times annually

Advanced Wage and Salary Administration, two days, offered four times annually

International Business

Managing International Joint Ventures, three days, offered twice annually

Negotiating with the Japanese, three days, offered twice annually

Labor Relations

Negotiating and Administering the Labor Contract, one week, offered four times annually

Strategic Collective Bargaining, one week, offered twice annually

Employee Discipline and Grievance Handling, two days, offered twice annually

How to Prepare and Win More Arbitration Cases, two days, offered twice annually

Marketing

Marketing for the Non-Marketing Manager, one week, offered three times annually

Strategic Marketing Planning, one week, offered four times annually

New Products Management: How to Set up New Product Programs, one week, offered three times annually

Business-to-Business Marketing Strategies, one week, offered twice annually

Effective Sales Management, three days, offered three times annually

Strategies in Sales Management for Sales Executives, three days, offered four times annually

Applied Methods in Marketing Research, one week, offered twice annually

Sample Courses

Managing International Joint Ventures. This three-day seminar is designed to suggest ways for executives to advance existing global competitive strategies and to open pathways to new markets. The program is targeted towards managers responsible for the formulation and implementation of their firms' global competitive strategies who are considering joint ventures with foreign firms as one of their strategic options.

The Michigan Business School identifies the following as benefits of attending the course. Participants will:

Identify sources of global competitive advantage

Analyze the role of joint ventures and other strategic alliances in the competitive strategies of potential overseas partners

Acquire an analytical framework for weighing the advantages and disadvantages of engaging in joint ventures or other cooperative arrangements with foreign firms

Apply the analytical framework to both traditional markets, like Europe and Japan, and non-traditional markets like China

Deepen their understanding of the strategic implications of various forms of cooperative agreements

Review case studies of past joint ventures that reveal why some were successful while others failed

Identify criteria for selecting a viable joint venture partner and discover or reaffirm the importance of synergy

Review the process of negotiating and setting up a long-term cooperative venture

Determine costs and benefits of various forms of strategic alliance and which are right for their firm

Enhance their understanding of the design requirements for management and control structures in joint ventures that will protect their long-term competitive position

Review human resource policies that make for a successful joint venture and discover techniques to manage cross-cultural differences

An outline of the seminar is as follows:

Day 1

- Strategic Alliances as a Management Process

  Introduction: cooperative strategies and global competition
  Successes and failures of past joint venture activities
  Defending competitive advantage: ownership vs. control
  Joint ventures as a strategy for learning

- Partner Selection and Negotiations

  The selection criteria and guidelines
  The logic of partner selection (case study)
  The fundamentals of the negotiation process
  Equity distribution and board competition
  (Evening: Legal issues in joint venture strategies)

Day 2

- Implementation of Joint Venture Strategies
  Strategic perspective of JV management
  Cost and benefits of international alliances
  Design choices for joint ventures
  Managing networks of strategic alliances (case study)

■ Joint Ventures in Non-Traditional Markets

Economic environment in non-traditional markets
Managing relations with the host government
Joint ventures in China: issues and guidelines
Lessons for Western firms
(Evening: Doing business in Eastern Europe)

Day 3

■ Critical Tasks in Joint Venture Management

Protecting synergy and long-term interest
Developing competencies through strategic partnerships
Effective learning techniques for joint ventures
Controlling distribution of benefits

■ Management Processes in Joint Venture Firms

Human resource policies for successful joint ventures
Managing cross-cultural interactions
The roles of top management (parent and JV)
Program summary: fundamentals of success

Negotiating with the Japanese. This three-day seminar is designed to teach participants how to negotiate more effectively with Japanese executives. The school identifies the following as benefits for participants. They will:

Gain insight into the cultural characteristics and business practices that structure the Japanese approach to negotiations

Learn to recognize and respond to specific Japanese negotiating techniques and practices

Meet and interact with executives who will share their firsthand knowledge and experience of dealing with the Japanese

Take part in simulated negotiations with Japanese nationals

The course is targeted towards managers and executives responsible for dealing with Japanese firms who must formulate negotiating strategies, conduct negotiations or implement agreements reached with their Japanese counterparts.

Topics covered include:

- Negotiational Theory

  What are the different types of negotiators you have to be able to deal with?

  What are the different dimensions that negotiators proceed along?

- Communicating with the Japanese

  What does "yes" mean in a Japanese context and what are the substitutes for "no"?

  How do you read their body language and how will they read yours?

  How should you handle criticism and compliments?

  What are the costs and benefits of negotiating in English or using an interpreter?

- Preparation

  When you sit down at the table, your Japanese counterparts will have done their homework carefully. If you hope to deal with them on even terms, you'd better have done yours as well. This section looks at what bases participants must cover in advance.

- The Negotiations Themselves

  How to manage the negotiation process itself

  What will be going on at the table and away from it

  What sort of follow-up you should build into the agreement

- Negotiating Styles: Ours and Theirs

  What particular difficulties are imposed by the disparity between American and Japanese negotiating styles?

  What pitfalls should you be aware of and how can you avoid them?

- Simulated Negotiations

  Based on case information and roles assigned in advance, participants will negotiate with a team of Japanese executives representing a fictitious company.

Leonard N. Stern School of Business
New York University
Office of Academic Advising
100 Trinity Place
New York, NY 10006
Tel: (212) 285-6245

Advanced Professional
Certificate Program

In this program, executives take a series of modules consisting of advanced courses offered by the Leonard N. Stern School of Business.

The Advanced Professional Certificate
in Accounting and Federal Taxation

Module I: Financial Reporting Option

Module II: Financial Management and Reporting Option

Module III: CPA Professional Program

Module IV: Federal Taxation Option

Module V: International Marketing Option

The Advanced Professional Certificate
in Management and Organizational
Behavior

Module I: General Management

Module II: Corporate Strategy

Module III: Organizational Analysis

The Advanced Professional Certificate
in Marketing

Module I: Marketing Management

Module II: Behavioral Sciences in Marketing

Module III: Marketing for Financial Institutions

Module IV: Retail Management

Module V: Product Management

Module VI: Marketing Research

Module VII: Analysis of Marketing Data

The Advanced Professional Certificate
in International Business

Module I: International Accounting Option

Module II: International Economics Option

Module III: International Finance Option

Module IV: International Management Option

*The Advanced Professional Certificate
in Statistics and Operations Research*

Module I: Survey of Statistics and Operation Research

Module II: Basic Statistics and Operations Research Option

Module III: Advanced Statistics and Operations Research Program

Statistics Option
Mathematical Programming Option
Operations Research Models Option

*General Advanced Professional
Certificate*

The Visiting Professionals Program

This program enables students holding MBAs or other advanced degrees to take advanced graduate courses at the Leonard N. Stern School of Business.

*The Advanced Professional Certificate
in Actuarial Science*

*The Advanced Professional Certificate
in Economics*

Module I: Business Conditions Analysis

Module II: Econometric Modeling and Forecasting

Module III: Managerial Economics

Module IV: Advanced Managerial Economics

Module V: Financial Economics

*The Advanced Professional Certificate
in Finance*

Module I: Corporate Financial Management

Module II: Investment Management

Module III: Management of Financial Institutions

*The Advanced Professional Certificate
in Information Systems*

**Sloan School of Management
Executive Programs**

Massachusetts Institute of Technology
Room E52-126
50 Memorial Drive
Cambridge, MA 02139
Tel: (617) 253-7168
Fax: (617) 258-6002

Executive Education Programs

Alfred P. Sloan Fellows Program, twelve months master's program

MIT Program for Senior Executives, eight weeks, offered once annually

MIT Management of Technology Program, twelve months master's program

Special Executive Education Programs

Corporate Strategy, one week, offered once annually

Financial Management, one week, offered once annually

Management of Change in Complex Organizations, one week, offered once annually

Negotiation: Theory & Practice, one week, offered once annually

System Dynamics: Microcomputer Simulation of Corporate Strategy and Social Systems, one week, offered once annually

Japanese Technology Management (not offered in 1993)

Management Issues for Corporate Counsel (not offered in 1993)

Sample Courses

The MIT Management of Technology Program. This one-year program, beginning in June and offered jointly by the Sloan School of Management and the MIT School of Engineering, leads to the degree of Master of Science in the Management of Technology. The program is designed to help prepare mid-career executives for senior management of technological and manufacturing resources.

The program is targeted towards those possessing engineering or science backgrounds and a minimum of five years' work experience with either a private or public sector organization. The curriculum was designed expressly for scientists and engineers who have been in the field for eight to twelve years and anticipate increased managerial responsibilities on the technical and manufacturing side of the organization. This one-year program is structured around three integrated elements:

1. Core, background subjects in analytical methods drawn from the disciplines of engineering, statistics, mathematics, economics and the behavioral sciences
2. Analysis of the theories, concepts and practice of managing technology-based organizations; organizational integration of innovative design and production systems; and the management of technical professionals
3. An original thesis under faculty consultation in the area of technology or manufacturing management

Curriculum Overview

Summer Term

Financial and Management Accounting and Control

Applied Micro- and Macroeconomic Theory

Decision Support System II

Dynamic Strategic Planning

Managing Professionals

Fall Term

Managing Technology

Strategic Management of Technology

The R&D Process: Communications and Organization

Marketing Management

Seminar in the Management of Technology

Plus at least one graduate-level elective

The January Field Trip

Spring Term

Corporate Strategies for Managing Research, Development and Engineering

Financial Management

Seminar in the Management of Technology

Plus thesis and at least one graduate-level elective

Participants must take at least one course in manufacturing; other elective choices include:

Government and the management of technology

Negotiation theory and practice

Negotiation and conflict management

Project management

Technology strategy

Economics for technology strategy

International business management

The management of research

Assessment of emerging technologies

The MIT Executive Program in Management of Change in Complex Organizations. This intensive, one-week program provides a research-based perspective on a number of emerging managerial problems and considers the various ways these problems can and should be addressed. The focus is on issues with wide applicability across organizations, national boundaries and technical domains.

The program targets general managers or high-level functional managers for whom coordinating the efforts of diverse groups in an organization is a daily concern. Staff executives responsible for up-to-date management training and education may also profit from the program. The number of participants is limited.

Teaching methods include morning lectures and discussions as well as afternoon workshops where participants discuss the morning's materials in detail. Afternoon sessions make use of case studies, problem-solving exercises, small group discussions and role-playing tasks. Themes examined include:

- Changes in managerial thought and practice
- New perspectives on managerial decision making
- The management of task forces, project teams and temporary groups
- Managing diversity in the organization

- Managing organizational change
- Diagnosing organization culture(s) and the process of cultural change

Specific topics addressed are:

- Work in contemporary society
- Managing a diverse work force
- Managing organizational conflict
- Strategies of negotiation in organizations
- Introducing new technology
- Restructuring and technological change
- Individual decision making
- Information technology and managerial decision making; management flight simulator
- Organization culture of large firms

Office of Executive Education
Graduate School of Business
Stanford University
Stanford, CA 94305-5015
Tel: (415) 723-3341
Fax: (415) 723-3950

Stanford Executive Program (eight weeks)

Functional Programs (one to two weeks): topics include organizational change, financial management, international investment management, marketing and others

Executive Programs

Stanford Executive Program, seven weeks, offered once annually

Executive Program for Smaller Companies, two weeks, offered twice annually

Financial Management Program, two weeks, offered once annually

Marketing Management: A Strategic Perspective, two weeks, offered once annually

Executive Program in Organization Change, two weeks, offered once annually

Strategic Executive Program in Mexico, three weeks, offered once annually

Executive Program in Singapore, three weeks, offered once annually

Executive Program in Strategy and Organization, two weeks, offered once annually

Sample Courses

Stanford Executive Program. Designed for busy senior executives, this seven-week program provides senior executives with the opportunity to think about their role in the strategic direction of their organizations and to learn, regenerate and grow. For the seven weeks of the program, executives are separated from office, telephone and the pressures of daily work, providing the requisite time, intellectual stimulation and freedom to prepare them for the more complex managerial challenges that lie ahead.

The program is designed to achieve several broad objectives. These are to:

Broaden the manager's strategic perspective on the complex and integrative nature of general management

Increase insight into the management process, advancing understanding of organizational behavior and leadership theory

Systematically update knowledge of the functional areas of business, including finance, accounting and marketing

Sharpen decision-making ability by improving both qualitative and quantitative judgment through modern methods of analysis

Develop a framework for understanding the impact both of the national and international environments and of changing social, political and economic factors on the success of the enterprise

Stimulate fresh thinking through exposure to new ideas

Encourage reexamination of personal goals and values

The program targets senior-level executives from throughout the world whose careers have been marked by success and considerable achievement. In most cases, participants are general managers, one or two levels below the chief executive officer. Some are senior-level executives responsible for specific functional areas such as marketing, production, finance, legal services, human resources and research and development. CEOs and vice presidents of rapidly growing smaller companies are also welcome. Participants represent a wide variety of firms, industries and nationalities, generally range in age from 40 to 55 and possess an average of 15 years of managerial experience.

Stanford uses a variety of teaching methods in the course of the program including lectures and discussion, the case method, small groups, workshops and informal interaction among participants. In addition, participants are encouraged to share ideas and experiences with peers, all of whom are experienced senior managers drawn from a wide variety of businesses and public organizations throughout the world.

Topics covered include the following:

- Strategic Management

  Business strategy and growth of the firm
  Industry structure and dynamics
  Strategic change and evaluation of strategic options
  Acquisitions and strategic alliances
  Corporate and division level strategy
  Organization design and culture
  Strategic issues in managing for total quality
  Strategic challenges for the 1990s

- Managing the International Business

  Forces of globalization and regionalism in international business
  Globalization and industry evolution
  Achieving responsiveness and flexibility in the international firm
  Host government and multinational interests in developing countries

- Management Control and Financial Reporting

  Accounting for management control
  Analysis of cost-volume relationships
  Financial accounting and corporate reports
  Inflation accounting and consolidation
  Relevant cost analysis
  Profit planning and budgeting
  Divisional performance measurement
  International financial reporting

Accounting for quality

- Organizational Behavior

  Managerial thinking and organizational culture
  Leadership
  Managing conflict
  Organizational structure, productivity and morale
  Managing high-performance teams
  Corporate strategy and human resources practices
  Alternative ownership forms and work arrangements
  Compensation and performance
  Managing with diversity

- The World Economic Environment

  Productivity, competitiveness and growth
  External balance, international trade and capital flows
  Economic convergence in the twentieth century
  The world economy in the twenty-first century
  Changing roles of Europe, the US and Japan in the world economy

- Macroeconomic Analysis and Policy

  Macroeconomic forces shaping the US economy
  Growth and fluctuation of economic aggregates
  Monetary policy and capital markets
  Productivity, competitiveness and growth

- Marketing Management

  Analyzing customers: management implications
  Forces of change in distribution
  The marketing mix: pricing policy
  Product transition
  Organizing and implementing the marketing effort

- Finance

  Financial analysis and funds requirements
  Balanced financial growth
  Capital budgeting with foreign exchange risk
  Valuation, rates of return and competitive advantage
  Capital structure and debt financing

Coping with financial distress
Corporate restructuring
World financial markets

- Business, Government and the Environment

    The public policy environment of business
    Public opinion, interest groups and corporate responsibility
    Market intervention and regulation
    Business interests, ethics and the political process
    Business and government in Japan and Europe

- Corporate Governance

    Fiduciary duties of officers and directors
    Allocation of power between directors and shareholders
    Effective boards of directors
    Executive compensation systems

Strategic Executive Program in Mexico. This three-week program, offered at Stanford's Monterrey Institute of Technology in Mexico, is an intensive course designed to enrich the management skills of senior executives and allow them to work more effectively in an increasingly complex international environment. The curriculum places a special emphasis on new opportunities for cooperation and trade in the North American region.

The program is designed to accomplish the following:

Broaden the managerial perspective and enhance the organizational effectiveness of upper-level managers

Introduce emerging new ideas and perspectives in the basic functional areas of management, including accounting, economics, finance, manufacturing, marketing and organizational behavior

Focus on the advancing integration of business in North America and its implications for managing in the competitive global environment

Offer mangers the opportunity to work with and get to know a diverse group of executives from Mexico, the United States and Canada.

The program targets applicants with significant management experience (usually ten years or more) who are at a senior level in their organizations. All participants must be sponsored by their employers and must be proficient in the English language.

Teaching methods include lectures, class discussions, case studies and small group discussions.
Topics covered include the following:

- Political and cultural environment
- Business and marketing strategies
- Organizational design and change
- Economic and regulatory issues
- Management of financial resources
- Modern manufacturing practices

Thunderbird
American Graduate School of International Management
15249 N. 59th Avenue
Glendale, AZ 85306-3399
Tel: (602) 978-7210
Fax: (602) 439-5432

Executive Programs (one to two weeks): topics include international financing concepts, practical solutions for foreign exchange problems, globalization, corporate strategy, human resources management, cross-cultural communication and implementation problems and others; Advanced Management Program for Oil and Gas Company Managers (two weeks); a newly created Executive Master of International Management Degree Program (two years) will provide instruction in modern languages, international studies and world business.

Executive Master of International Management Degree

Advanced Management Program for Agribusiness Industry Managers, one week, offered once annually

Advanced Management Program for Oil and Gas Company Managers, two weeks, offered once annually

Finance, Accounting and Control for Oil and Gas Company Managers, one week, offered twice annually

Financial Issues in Global Firms, one week, offered twice annually

Globalization: Merging Strategy with Action, one week, offered twice annually

Custom-Designed Programs

TMC provides custom-designed seminars and training programs for individuals, companies, associations, and government agencies. These programs vary widely in content and can range anywhere from two days to thirty weeks. Most longer programs are taught on campus, however programs of up to two weeks can be held anywhere on earth. Professors include faculty of the American Graduate School of International Management as well as experts from other institutions.

All courses have an international dimension. Topics are drawn from three main areas: Cross-Cultural Communication and Regional Studies, Language Skills and International Management.

Thunderbird lists the following topics as being representative of those covered in custom-designed programs:

- International Management

  Countertrade and Sourcing
  Global Business Policies
  Industry Analysis
  Insurance and Risk Management
  International Consumer Marketing
  International Corporate Financial Management
  International Economics
  International Finance and Trade
  International Industrial Marketing
  Managing in a Global Context: Both Manufacturing and Service
  Operations Management
  Technology Transfer

- Export Development

  Distribution Channels
  Export Marketing
  Financing Export Transactions
  Foreign Dealer Legislation
  U.S. Export Tax Strategies

- Cross-Cultural Issues

  Cross-Cultural Negotiations
  Cross-Cultural Orientation Programs
  Cultural Awareness Training

Managing Cultural Differences
Managing in a Foreign Environment

- Contemporary Business in Major Economic Regions
  Asia
  Europe
  Latin America
  Middle East

- Intensive Language Training in nearly a dozen languages

Sample Courses

Financial Issues in Global Firms. Designed to enable global managers to master the financial side of global competition, this week-long course focuses on issues arising from globalization.

The course is designed to let participants learn how to apply the successful financial strategies of other firms to their own, become familiar with the workings of the foreign exchange market, understand how certain foreign exchange exposures can be managed through financing, sourcing or selling decisions, learn how cross-border considerations enter into a well-executed capital expenditure analysis process, study alternative funding strategies in the context of foreign exchange and interest rate uncertainty, analyze and discuss concrete case histories on relevant financial aspects of global firms, learn how performance measurement systems do and do not need to incorporate international considerations, draw on the knowledge of an experienced team of experts, learn practical concepts and techniques that they can use immediately.

Topics covered include:

- Global Financial System
  The institutional structure
  Euro-currency financial products
  Trends in world financial markets

- Fundamentals of Exchange Rates
  Environmental causes and factors
  Equilibrium conditions
  Alternative currency systems

- Foreign Exchange Needs and Products

  Types of foreign exchange exposure
  Managing foreign exchange risk
  Matching products with needs

- Financial Forecasting and Analysis

  Effects of inflation
  Effects of multinational competition
  Projecting and assessing needs

- International Investment Analysis

  Foreign direct investment
  Capital expenditure analysis
  Cross-currency effects

- Performance Measurement Systems

  Management control systems
  Transfer pricing issues

Globalization: Merging Strategy with Action. Designed to address the many differences that distinguish competition on a global basis from that domestically, this week-long course is designed to give managers a deeper and more useful understanding of the essential concepts of competing in a global environment. The primary objective of the seminar is to help the individual participants to become better general managers in a world of global competition. A secondary objective is to expose participants to a more comprehensive view of global competition.

Thunderbird describes benefits to participants as follows. They will:

Master essential concepts of global strategy

Learn how other firms have dealt with issues of global competition

Become more aware of how their own culture shapes values, priorities and expectations

Increase their ability to manage cultural differences among and within organizations

Understand the key issues surrounding the design of a global manufacturing strategy

Understand the competitive role of human resource management in a global strategy

Analyze issues of organizational structure and process in a global firm

Use industry and competitor analysis techniques to assess a competitive situation

Draw on the knowledge of an experienced team of global professors and consultants

Learn concepts and techniques that will have an immediate effect on professional performance

Topics covered include:

- Strategic Implementation
  Industry and competitor analysis
  Negotiated market structure
  Organizational structure and process

- Strategy in Global Industries
  Globalization of markets
  Assessing competitive risks
  Strategy development

- International Operations Management
  Global manufacturing strategies
  Technology transfer issues
  Manufacturing as a competitive weapon

- Cross-Cultural Communication
  Influence of culture on management behavior
  Cross-cultural leadership, communication and motivation
  Analysis and application

- International Human Resource Management
  Human resources as a competitive weapon
  Developing the international manager
  Issues of expatriates and repatriation

The Amos Tuck School of Business Administration
Dartmouth College
Hanover, NH 03755-1798
Tel: (603) 646-2839
Fax: (603) 646-1308

Tuck Executive Program, four weeks, offered once annually

MBA: Update 2000 Module 1, one week, offered twice annually

Leveraging Core Competencies, four days, offered twice annually

Implementing Strategy, one week, offered twice annually

MBA: Update 2000 Module 2, one week, offered once annually

Effective Management of Production Operations, one week, offered once annually

Marketing Strategy, one week, offered once annually

Minority Business Executive Program, one week, offered once annually

Sample Courses

Tuck Executive Program. This four-week program is designed to provide senior managers with new ideas and fresh approaches to the challenges facing business today. The intensive program integrates a study of major business disciplines within the context of strategic management.

The principal objectives of the program are as follows. It is designed to:

Broaden executives' understanding of the integrative nature of general management by identifying the key management issues in each of the functional areas from a general manager's perspective

Enhance executives' abilities to formulate and implement strategies to gain global competitive advantage

Increase executives' abilities to anticipate and respond to critical management challenges facing their firms and provide the opportunity for the transfer of "best practices"

Sharpen executives' skills in initiating and managing organizational change

The program is targeted towards an experienced group of executives from leading corporations around the world. Participants are typically heads of functional areas, newly appointed general managers and country managers. They have approximately, on average, fifteen years of management experience and make decisions that affect two or more functional areas.

The program is organized according to several themes. It examines key management issues in functional areas from the point of view of a general manager. It also focuses on issues that require cross-functional integration including managing new product development, managing total quality and managing global strategies. In addition, the program integrates leading-edge concepts such as leveraging core competencies and managing intellectual assets with the accompanying leadership, teamwork, communication and negotiation skills required to lead twenty-first century organization. The program uses simulated business environments. Finally, its emphasis is on current challenges, including "best practices" of benchmarked companies.

The following gives a description of the content of the course by week.

Week 1

- Developing a General Manager's Perspective

  Strategy formulation and implementation
  Marketing management
  Financial management
  Human resource management
  Operations management
  Strategic cost management
  Corporate communications

Week 2

- Managing Cross-Functional Integration

  Managing globalization and global strategies
  Managing technology
  Integrating acquisitions
  Managing new product development
  Creating strategic alliances
  Managing total quality

Week 3

- Building Adaptive Organizations

  Leveraging core competencies
  Designing network organizations
  Leading twenty-first century organizations
  Managing intellectual assets
  Managing teams

Initiating and managing organizational change

Week 4

- Synthesis: Addressing Current Management Challenges

Application and integration of key concepts through a business simulation

Team presentation of "best practices" on critical management challenges facing executives and their companies

Development of action plans for the executives' transfer of individual learning back to their organization

Implementing Strategy Program. The focus of this one-week seminar is on planning, organization design and human resource decisions that are critical to the successful implementation of strategy. The practical, action-oriented program develops a logical model of key implementation activities. Emphasis is on understanding the important steps or decisions in the implementation process. Upon completion of this seminar, participants should be better able to identify the structural and planning decisions that affect the attainment of strategic objectives.

The principal objectives of the course are to enable participants to do the following:

Understand how strategic choices and formulation activities affect the implementation process

Lean how to integrate the short and long term in implementing strategy

Learn how to avoid the "mistakes" in incentives and controls that hurt long-run performance

Understand how strategy affects organization design

Recognize what must be done to manage strategic change effectively

The program uses a number of different learning methods including case studies, lectures/discussions and group exercises. Instructional materials include consumer, industrial, service and high-technology problems and emphasize a high-level strategic orientation.

The program is targeted towards executives with a minimum of ten years of experience in the following categories:

1. Individuals with general or strategic management responsibilities

2. Functional and operating managers responsible for important aspects of the implementation process

3. Managers who aspire to or are being groomed for general management positions

4. Managers who wish to learn how the implementation of strategy affects their jobs

5. Managers generally interested in understanding the factors that are central to the success of the implementation process

Aresty Institute of Executive Education
Wharton School
University of Pennsylvania
The Steinberg Conference Center
255 South 38th Street
Philadelphia, PA 19104-6359
Tel: (215) 898-4560
Fax: (215) 386-4304

Senior Management Programs

Wharton Advanced Management Program, five weeks, offered three times annually

The International Forum, one-week sessions, offered three times annually

Executive Development Program

Executive Development Program: The Transition from Functional to General Management, two weeks, offered twice annually

Finance and Accounting

Creating Value through Financial Management, one week, offered twice annually

Finance and Accounting for the Non-Financial Manager, one week, offered five times annually

Integrating Finance and Marketing: A Strategic Framework, one week, offered twice annually

Mergers and Acquisitions, one week, offered twice annually

Pension Funds and Money Management, one week, offered twice annually

Understanding and Applying SEC and FASB Reporting Requirements, four days, offered twice annually

Management

Corporate Restructuring for Results: A Management Perspective, one week, offered twice annually

Corporate Venturing: Developing Successful New Businesses In-House, one week, offered twice annually

Fundamentals of Market-Driven Business Planning, one week, offered twice annually

Implementing Strategy, one week, offered twice annually

Managing Organizational Change, one week, offered twice annually

Managing People: Effectiveness through Individual and Group Dynamics, four days, offered twice annually

Managing Technology and Innovation, one week, offered twice annually

The Next Generation of Family Members in Family-Held Businesses, one week, offered twice annually

Strategic Alliances, four days, offered twice annually

Strategic Thinking and Management for Competitive Advantage, one week, offered twice annually

Marketing

Advanced Industrial Marketing Strategy, one week, offered twice annually

Building and Leveraging Brand Equity, one week, offered twice annually

Competitive Marketing Strategy, one week, offered twice annually

Integrating Finance and Marketing: A Strategic Framework, one week, offered twice annually

New Product Development and Introduction, one week, offered twice annually

Sales Force Management, one week, offered twice annually

Strategies for Complex Negotiations, one week, offered twice annually

Quality and Service

Benchmarking Strategy and Techniques, four days, offered twice annually

Creating World-Class Capabilities, four days, offered twice annually

Managing Services: Reengineering for Quality, one week, offered twice annually

Industry-Specific Programs (offered in 1993)

Although organized in conjunction with other schools, associations, companies or financial institutions around the world, these courses are normally open to the public. A few, however, are by invitation only. Most take place at the facilities of the co-sponsoring organization which are often located outside the US.

The ABA Trust and Private Banking Executive Management School, five days, offered once annually

Institute for Group Practice Executives, four days, offered once annually

The Institute of Secured Lending, two weeks, offered once annually

The Wharton-Nomura Financial Management Program, two weeks, offered once annually

Petroleum Management: Executive Session, three weeks, offered once annually

The Nomura Investment Management Program, two weeks, offered once annually

Insurance Agency Management in Turbulent Times, five days, offered once annually

Certified Investment Management Analysis Program, five days, offered once annually

Securities Industry Institute, five days, offered once annually

Advanced Asset/Liability Management of Life Insurers, three days, offered once annually

Fundamentals of Money Management, five days, offered once annually

The Advanced Executive Education Program, two weeks, offered twice annually

Customized Programs

Tailored to meet the needs of individual companies, customized programs can be developed on virtually any subject and normally run from three days to five weeks. Flexibility is a major feature. Multiweek programs are designed to be spread over several months to allow for integration of classroom material with on-the-job experiences. Learning methods include traditional lectures, case studies, computer simulations, management games, back-at-work projects and lectures by senior company management.

Sample Courses

Strategies for Negotiation in International Markets. Offered twice annually, this six-day course covers a wide variety of negotiations issues. Those taking the course explore a wide range of negotiations— between two individuals, between two firms, between a firm and a host government, multiparty negotiations and coalition formation.

The program is designed to enable participants to develop the analytical tools necessary to put together a strategy for successful negotiations, refine their negotiating style, improve communication skills, gain an appreciation of the intercultural factors that play a critical role in negotiating successfully with parties in other countries and learn about state-of-the-art computer tools designed to enhance negotiating effectiveness.

Besides studying techniques, participants also practice negotiating against one another with the aid of video recorders.

Session topics include the following:

- Fundamentals of Negotiations

  Characteristics common to negotiations

  The basics of distributive negotiations (negotiations conducted to gain competitive advantage)

  The basics of interactive negotiations (where a "win-win" outcome is desirable)

  Cross-cultural issues

- Complex Negotiations

  Negotiations involving more than two parties

  Forming coalitions

  Negotiations involving multiple issues

  Arbitration and mediation

- Strategic Planning

  Preparing for effective negotiations
  Gathering and analyzing information
  Developing an appropriate communication approach
  Adopting the appropriate behavioral approach

- Experiencing Different Types of Negotiations

  Negotiating in person
  Negotiating by computer, fax or mail

- Some Lessons from the Real World

  Case-study analyses of successful and unsuccessful negotiations

The Transition from Functional to General Management. Offered twice annually, this twelve-day course is designed for managers who have graduated from a function role to a position covering more than one functional area or international region. Those taking the course are taught to lead groups across different functional or regional borders. During the intensive two-week program, managers from a wide range of backgrounds, along with experts from diverse fields, get together to address the challenges of leading cross-functional teams. Through interactive sessions, lectures, business simulations and personal feedback on leadership styles, they gain useful experience that will help them make the leap to general management.

The course is designed to enable participants to develop the professional and interpersonal skills needed to lead multifunctional teams, expand and deepen their knowledge of functional areas outside their own, strengthen confidence and their ability to make decisions, devise practical plans of action to tackle important issues when they return to work and broaden their world view by association with managers from a variety of other industries, countries and cultures. Typically more than 30% of participants are from overseas and a wide variety of backgrounds insures that participants will be exposed to executives from finance, operations management, marketing and other functions.

Topics covered include:

- Team development
- Financial management
- Operations management

- Marketing management
- Conflict management
- Managing technology and innovation
- Designing, integrating and innovating organizations
- Managing new product and service development
- Strategic use of information systems
- Managing change with ambiguous authority
- Managing the multinational firm
- Confronting the leadership challenge

Appendix **B**

Select
Middle-Management
and Board Level
Programs

Select Middle-Management Programs, Class Size and Composition

School	Program	Class size	International partici-pants (%)
	Europe		
Ashridge	International Managers' Program	18	50
Ashridge	Management-Development Program	32–36	—
Cranfield	General Management for Specialists	17–20	20–25
Cranfield	Management-Development Program	5–17	15
IMD	Program for Executive Development	50	—
Insead	Insead International Executive Program	45	High
Irish Management Institute	Executive Development Program	—	Mainly nationals
London Business School	Accelerated Development Program	45	45
	United States		
California, Berkeley	Executive Program	60	40
Carnegie-Mellon	Program for Executives	39	25
Cornell	Executive Development Program	60–70	30
Harvard	Program for Management Development	135	50
Hawaii	International Business Program	30	—
Houston	Executive Development Program	30–35	33
Illinois	Executive Development Program	30–35	—
Michigan	Executive Program	55–60	25
New Hampshire	Executive Development Program	25	—
Kellogg	Executive Development Program	60	30
Pennsylvania State	Program for Executive Development	42	33
Pittsburgh	Management Program for Executives	30	—
Virginia	The Executive Program	100–104	25

SOURCE: *Developing Managers: A Guide to Executive Programmes in Europe and the US*, Special Report No. 1200, The Economist Publications, 1990.

Select Senior-Management Programs, Class Size and Composition

School	Program	Class size	International participants (%)
	Europe		
Ashridge	Strategic Management Program	20–24	—
Bradford	Senior Executive Program	16	All UK
Cranfield	Senior Managers' Program	24	20
IMD	Seminar for Senior Executives	50	—
IMD	Managing Corporate Resources	50	—
IMD	International Executive Program	50	—
Insead	Advanced Management Program	70	—
London Business School	The Senior Executive Program	40	42
	United States		
Columbia	Executive Program in Int'l Management	50	60
Columbia	Executive Program in Business Administration	70	40
Harvard	Advanced Management Program	80	40
Harvard	International Senior Management Program	80–100	90
Kellogg	International Advanced Executive Program	20	50
Kellogg	Advanced Executive Program	60	30
Pennsylvania State	Executive Management Program	46	26
Sloan School	Program for Senior Executives	50	20
Southern California	Executive Program	30–40	30
Stanford	Executive Program	60	45
Amos Tuck	Tuck Executive Program	80	—
Wharton	Advanced Management Program	40	60

SOURCE: *Developing Managers: A Guide to Executive Programmes in Europe and the US,* Special Report No. 1200, The Economist Publications, 1990.

Select European and US Board-Level Programs and Class Size

School	Program	Class size
Ashridge	Directors' Program	12–16
Henley	The Directors' Workshop	15–20
IMD	International Program for Senior Executives	45
IMD	International Program for Board Members	15–25
Insead	Managing Multinational Enterprises	25
Wharton	The International Forum	30

SOURCE: *Developing Managers: A Guide to Executive Programmes in Europe and the US,* Special Report No. 1200, The Economist Publications, 1990.

Appendix **C**

Selected Cross-Cultural Resources in the US

American Society for Training and Development (ASTD)
1640 King Street, Box 1443
Alexandria, VA 22313
Contact: Curtis E. Plott
Tel: (703) 683-8100
Fax: (703) 683-8103

Established in 1944, the ASTD is the world's largest professional association in the field of employee training. It represents more than 55,000 managers, administrators, educators and others who design and implement training and development programs for the work force. The society recently comple ted a three-year study on the best practices in training, in the course of which it gathered an extensive body of data. In general, the organization works to publicize the importance of training and makes recommendations on training solutions to business, as well as government.

Business Council for International Understanding (BCIU)
The American University
3301 New Mexico Avenue, N.W., Ste 244
Washington, DC 20016
Contact: Gary Lloyd
Tel: (202) 686-2771
Fax: (202) 686-5923

Since 1958, the BCIU Institute at the American University in Washington, D.C. has educated and trained US citizens and foreign nationals to operate in other cultures. With over 25,000 graduates, from technicians to corporate CEOs in 148 countries, it has a long history. Eighty percent of the firm's programs are conducted in Washington, 20% on-site or overseas. Programs are custom designed for each company and are directed toward corporate staff, negotiating teams, departing expatriates and their families and reentering families, as well as foreigners coming to the US. Programs can range from one day to several weeks. As a part of its cross-cultural training, BCIU offers instruction in a wide variety of languages.

Center for Creative Leadership
5000 Laurinda Drive
P.O. Box 26300

Greensboro, NC 27438-6300
Contact: Pat Wegner
Tel: (919) 545-2810
Fax: (919) 288-3999

Founded in 1970, the Center for Creative Leadership is a nonprofit educational institution with locations in Greensboro, North Carolina, Colorado Springs, Colorado, San Diego, California and Brussels, Belgium. The center offers a wide variety of management workshops and programs in executive leadership, innovation and creativity, leadership development, leadership technologies and the education and nonprofit sectors. Some 16,000 participants take its courses annually, both as individuals and as groups. Besides more traditional courses, the center offers programs that emphasize interpersonal awareness, rapid change in the workplace and other topics, using methods partially derived from the study of the behavioral sciences. In addition to teaching courses itself, the center has a worldwide network of licensee/associates that offer its Leadership Development Program and other services.

Clarke Consulting Group Inc (CCG)
Three Lagoon Drive, Ste 230
Redwood City, CA 94065
Contact: Laurie Mack
Tel: (415) 591-8100
Fax: (415) 591-8269

Founded in 1980 as an outgrowth of the Stanford Institute for Intercultural Communication, CCG provides research-based intercultural consulting and training to executives of both US and Japanese firms. CCG offers client-tailored programs both at its training center in Redwood City, California, as well as at the client's facility. Training includes both long- and short-term programs in such areas as language and culture, intercultural business communications skill building, management team building, negotiation and relationship-building skills and reentry. CCG also facilitates technology transfer projects between Japanese and US companies from start-up to finish. In addition to training, the company offers consulting services in intercultural aspects of organizational development, strategic human resources development, international negotiation and leadership counseling.

Intercultural Communication Inc.
400 Second Avenue South, Ste 650
Minneapolis, MN 55401
Contact: Helen McNulty
Tel: (612) 333-6832

This firm provides several types of cross-cultural training, including programs on preparation for living and working overseas, expatriate reentry and life in the US for foreign nationals. The company also offers a program for executives who frequently travel overseas, as well as one on internationalizing the office. Each program is customized for the individual or group of individuals who will be trained, as well as for the company.

International Orientation Resources (IOR)
707 Skokie Boulevard, Ste 350
Northbrook, IL 60062
Contact: Kathline Seebert
Tel: (708) 205-0066
Fax: (708) 205-0085

IOR provides a variety of training services to a multinational client base, which includes large companies like Ciba-Geigy, Avery International, Ford Motor Corp and Siemens, as well as smaller clients just entering the global arena. Its different programs include predeparture cross-cultural training, overseas on-site orientation, intercultural business briefings, dual-career assistance, repatriation workshops, language programs and in-house program design. Though based in the US, the firm has offices or representation in more than 65 cities throughout the world.

TRI Psychological Resources
5225 Old Orchard Road, Ste 6
Skokie, IL 60077
Contact: Katherine Bloomfield
Tel: (708) 675-2280

Founded in 1986, TRI is a professional service firm specializing in human resources development for corporate transitions, relocations and intercultural assignments. The company's primary mission is to assist clients in effectively managing employee transfers, both domestically and internationally. Services include group-move programs, pre-departure preparation, repatriation, orientation of foreign nationals and spouse and family counseling. TRI structures programs lasting from three days to six weeks. Clients include Amoco, Arthur Andersen, Sara Lee and Hotel Sofitel.

Intercultural Resources Forum
LO*OP Center Inc.
760 Homer Avenue, Ste 3
Palo Alto, CA 94301
Contact: Liza Loop
Tel: (415) 322-6491
Fax: (415) 493-0622

The LO*OP Center offers several different services in the area of intercultural relations, including cross-cultural courses, seminars, retreats and workshops, which can range from a half day to several months. Courses are generally developed in conjunction with a client and address topics such as countering stereotypes and managing in culturally diverse settings, as well as dealing with culture shock and multicultural dispute resolution and avoidance. The center also helps match up companies with different consultants. Clients have included Apple, Ashton Tate and Grand Metropolitan Food.

Moran, Stahl & Boyer (MS&B)
International Division
900 28th Street
Boulder, CO 80303
Contact: Gary M. Wederspahn
Tel: (303) 449-8440
Fax: (303) 449-1064

MS&B, a subsidiary of The Prudential, provides a variety of services to a large, multinational client base, which includes General Motors, AT&T, Nippon Telephone and Telegraph, General Electric, Coca-Cola and others. Its expatriate and repatriate programs are custom designed for individual families and have been offered for over 25 years. MS&B also provides other services, including business globalization consulting, international human resources management design, expatriate assessment and selection, foreign language instruction, foreign business seminars, cross-cultural technology transfer, global interface skills training, intercultural video production, multicultural management and team building. MS&B has conducted programs covering 87 countries at its offices in Boulder, New York City, Tokyo and London, as well as at client locations worldwide.

Employee Relocation Council (ERC)
1720 N Street, N.W.
Washington, DC 20036
Contact: Anita Brienza
Tel: (202) 857-0857
Fax: (202) 467-4012

Founded in 1964, the ERC is a professional membership association of corporations concerned with employee transfer. Members of the Council include nearly 1,000 corporations, as well as 14,000 individuals and companies in the relocation industry. ERC programs and publications are designed to help relocation professionals increase their expertise and allow corporations that are transferring employees to share information and communicate more effectively.

Index

About the Author

THE ECONOMIST INTELLIGENCE UNIT, a wholly owned subsidiary
of the Economist Group, is a publishing and research firm
established to help companies initiate and maintain
operations across national borders. For 45 years, it has been a
source of information and know-how on worldwide business
and financial developments, economic and political trends,
government regulations, and corporate practice. In 1986, the
Economist Intelligence Unit merged with Business
International. Today, the company maintains a global
network of over 300 analysts, researchers, and editors in 95
countries. Through close-working relationships with top
corporate and government officials, the company analyzes
events and forecasts changes in the international business
environment with speed and accuracy and helps companies
take advantage of emerging opportunities in markets around
the world.

MICHAEL MOYNIHAN, the author, is a New York-based senior
consultant for the Economist Intelligence Unit for whom he
has written nine book and advises corporate and
government clients on cross-border topics. He also writes for
a variety of periodicals, including *Harper's* and *The
Washington Post*.